NOT SILENCED BY DARKNESS

by LARRY CLARK

The names of certain persons have been changed in order to protect their privacy.

Canadian Cataloguing in Publication Data

Clark, Larry, 1929-
Not silenced by darkness

ISBN 0-920479-20-0

1. Roman, Augustine. 2. Popoluca Indians - Biography. 3. Christian biography - Mexico. 4. Indians of Mexico - Biography. I. Title.
F1221.P6R65 1987 972'.00497 C87-091292-5

Second Printing 1992

Published by CREDO Publishing Corporation

ISBN 0-920479-20-0
(paperback)

Cover Design by Randy Watson
Illustration by Dale Cooper

CREDO Publishing Corporation
P.O. Box 3175
Langley, British Columbia
Canada V3A 4R5

Printed in the United States of America

God has made my heart faint;
the Almighty has terrified me;
Yet I am not silenced by the darkness,
by the thick darkness that covers my face.
Job 23:16,17 (NIV)

The Lord is my light and my salvation —
whom shall I fear?
Psalm 27:1 (NIV)

Table of Contents

Acknowledgments

I want to express appreciation to Hugh Steven, Wycliffe author and photographer-at-large who, fifteen years ago, encouraged me to write this story; to Roger Garland, Director of Communications at Wycliffe, who gave valuable guidance in the final stages of the manuscript; to Carol Chase and Terry Whalin, fellow writers with Wycliffe,who gave needed encouragement; to my wife, Nancy, who cheerfully worked behind the scenes and has been my best friend and companion; and above all, to the Coastal Popoluca people who, though unknown to the world, have enriched my life with their gracious and friendly ways.

Larry Clark
Huntington Beach, California

Prologue

Old buses and battered pick-up trucks cluttered the main street of Acayucan in southern Mexico. At the rear of each 1940-vintage bus, Mexican conductors stood and shouted their respective destinations—towns and villages with strange names, like Oluta, Jaltipan, and Sayula.

People known as Popolucas crowded onto the bus bound for their hometown of Sayula and shoved their bundles into overhead racks. As they jammed themselves into the metal seats, they chattered in their native language. The Mexican driver, used to the smooth flow of Spanish, grimaced; the rough indigenous words jarred his ears.

The bus climbed several roller-coaster hills and ten minutes afterward lurched to a halt in Sayula. The Popolucas jumped off and headed for their homes.

Beneath a broiling sun the Popoluca people had lived in isolation for centuries until a highway cut through the jungle in 1952 and catapulted them into modern times. The outside world made its impact in their village and one day two American men took up residence in a rented house with bamboo walls plastered with thick mud. Its red-tiled roof and cement floor distinguished it from the Indian homes with their palm thatch and dirt floors.

These outsiders wanted to learn the Popoluca language. This amazed the people—strangers had always scorned it. So the friendly Popolucas made the newcomers feel at home and taught them. They nicknamed one blond foreigner "Lencho Americano." Lencho is Spanish for Larry, and Americano is an affectionate term for "American."

But one cautious Popoluca steered clear of these intruders. Augustine Roman, driven by an angry temper, demanded something better for himself and his people. Outsiders had always exploited them. Lencho and his friend were probably no different.

Later, the Americano married and brought his bride, Nancy, to live among them. They really did mean to stay! Their home rested on a knoll overlooking a maze of houses and a sea of tropical forest that stretched into the horizon.

Augustine worked in that forest. This is his story.

CHAPTER 1

The Brick and Tile Maker

Great drops of perspiration rolled down Augustine's naked brown back. He cursed the fiery sun and glared at the hot brick oven in front of him. He reached for a bottle of warm coffee and half-emptied it in three lusty gulps. With a satisfied sigh he set the bottle in the shade of a gnarled tree and wiped his palms on the seat of his misshapen trousers. His energy sapped, he forced himself to keep on with the brutal work before him.

The sun poured out its heat. The Popoluca people had always endured scorching days, but this May afternoon in 1955 was different. Even old men of the Sayula village could not remember such an angry sun. Everyone longed for a rainstorm. Everyone, that is, except Augustine. Rain would snuff out the fire in his huge oven and ruin the firewood. No fire would mean no job.

The fierce heat struck him full in the face. Smoke filled his nostrils and forced him to turn away from the oven. He saw his older brother, Lino, lounging in the cool shade at the edge of the forest clearing, a bottle of sugarcane rum propped beside him.

Lino's dark face lit up with a grin while Augustine strained at the oven.

"How's the fire, Auguch?" (Augustine's family and close friends called him Auguch, an affectionate nickname.)

"Hot," Augustine answered. "Too hot when I have to watch it alone. You work here, too. Why don't you help me?"

Lino's grin widened. "I'm breaking you in. I worked three years by myself at that hot box and now it's your turn. You won't learn if I help you."

Annoyed, Augustine grumbled, "I can't do it alone. Wait'll the boss sees you lying on your back!"

Lino gazed fondly at his tall bottle of rum. Augustine followed his gaze and his mouth watered. No time for that, he thought. I've got to control myself.

Reclining in the grass, his back pushed up against a log, Lino uncorked the bottle, filling a gourd-cup with the "cooked water," as the Popolucas called their liquor. "Come have a drink," he yelled at Augustine.

Augustine trudged over to the shade. The dirt and sweat that begrimed him couldn't conceal his trim body, or his coal black hair above an alert face. He slumped beside his brother.

"Sorry, Lino. Rum drives me crazy. I can't drink and work, too. I need this job."

"Come on," Lino coaxed. "Forget the oven and have a drink."

Augustine shook his head and grabbed Lino's arm. Changing the subject, he asked, "Do you know what I saw today?"

Lino smiled. "No, what?"

"This morning I stood on a hilltop and looked out over our village with all its houses and thatch roofs. A few new ones had tile roofs. . . ."

"So what?" Lino wasn't impressed.

"Lino, you sour-brain! Those tile roofs mean we stay in business and make money."

Lino's lean face twitched with hidden laughter. "We roast ourselves at this furnace so people can have nice tile roofs? Hardly seems fair, brother."

Augustine glared at him. "I think past my belly, Lino. Someday tile roofs will cover all those huts. I'm going to master this work. Then our people won't have to live in simple homes. Sayula will have the best houses in Mexico."

"And I'll help," Lino remarked, "as long as the builders

give plenty of rum for my belly."

Anger pushed Augustine to his feet. "Forget it!" he snarled. Wiping the sweat from his face, he stomped back to the oven.

"I'm just joking," Lino called after him. "Can't you take it, little brother?" But he made no attempt to get up and help his brother, either.

Augustine turned his mind away from Lino and thought about his job. His boss let other Popolucas do the menial work. He chose me for the brain work, Augustine boasted to himself. Not many can arrange the bricks in the kiln and control the fire as well as I can!

He looked with pride at the fiery monster. It held 6,000 bricks in its adobe stomach, with strong walls built to withstand intense heat. But Augustine cast anxious glances at the weaker narrow opening in the center of the oven, now temporarily closed off with bricks and sealed with plaster The seal must remain perfect. One draft of cool air could ruin the bricks.

As Augustine inspected the oven wall, Lino sneaked up behind and yelled in his ear, "Do you like to eat smoke?"

Aside from a small reflex jump, Augustine ignored the comment. Why scold a clown? As he glanced away from Lino, suddenly a sharp jab of fear jolted him. A crack had appeared at the top of the oven wall and black smoke came gushing out.

"Quick, Lino!" he yelled. "Do something!"

Lino shot into action, In an instant he slammed a pole against the oven. Snatching up a handful of wet plaster, he scampered up the pole like a squirrel and slapped the plaster onto the fissure. His quick fingers worked it in until not even a wisp of smoke escaped. Just as quickly he clambered down the pole and stood in front of Augustine, a self-satisfied grin on his face.

"See? Nothing to get excited about."

Augustine felt foolish, but he clapped Lino on the back. "What quick work! Good thing you were right here. I can't climb a pole that fast."

The grin spread over Lino's face. Then he sneered at Augustine's work shoes, now scuffed and worn. "It's easy to climb poles 'cause I'm barefooted,' he said. "But you wear shoes, like city people."

Augustine ignored his pointed barb. "That wall break scared me. One gust of wind and two-weeks' work would have been gone! And we would be back weeding cornfields."

"Why worry?" Lino said. "We're a family and we work together. The boss told me he wanted more helpers. Did I get the first man I saw? No way. I got you, my kid brother. Don't worry so much."

Somehow Lino's words didn't help, but Augustine listened with respect. His father had drummed it into his head: the older bosses the younger. But it was hard not to worry.

"Lino, we've got a lot of work ahead. Let's get back to it."

"I know," Lino said, eyeing his bottle of rum. "This 'cooked water' will pull me through the next two days."

The afternoon wore on until the sun touched the horizon and the sky darkened. As the tropical night fell, Augustine slumped on a fallen log in the clearing and stared at the oven. A blast of flame lit up the night and illuminated the wall of trees around him.

Hemmed in by jungle, the night creatures silent, Augustine felt stark loneliness creeping into his spirit. His wife, Bella, and baby Tacho, drifted into his mind and sadness gripped him. Two more days till I go home, he reflected. But I've got to work. I can learn this trade and help my people.

Another flame burst from the oven and he stared at it. His ancestors had known only grass-roof huts, and palm thatch was no better when it caught on fire. Closing his eyes, Augustine dreamed of his jungle village—with rows of homes crowned with tile roofs.

CHAPTER 2

Raging Strong Drink

Augustine lay asleep on his stomach beside a fallen log until the heat from the noonday sun forced him to awaken. He brushed tangled hair out of his eyes and looked around. At first only some squawking parrots sounded in his ears, but finally the clearing, which stretched out to the forest wall, came into view. His brother, Lino, sat beside him, a set of beady eyes fixed on the smoke that rose from the oven.

"It's almost noon," Lino said.

"Noon! Did I sleep that long?"

Lino's answer came slowly. "Yeah. We can go home now."

"I was dead tired," Augustine said. "The last two days nearly killed me. Then that midnight-to-sunrise shift wore me out."

"Well, it's all over, Auguch. The bricks are baked and us, too. Let's go and sop it up at Lonco's Tavern. The boss said he'll buy the drinks."

Lonco's was the hub of life for most Popoluca males, but Lino's remark drew a frown from Augustine. "Lino, that's all you think about." He pulled himself up onto the log and sat beside his older brother. "Why drink that rotgut cane liquor? Someday it'll kill you."

"Don't worry," Lino replied. "The boss won't buy cheap stuff today. Let's go. The sun's burning me up."

Bone weary, the two men dragged themselves away from

the log. Augustine snatched his shirt off a tree branch and threw it on. Leaving it unbuttoned, he started off down the trail after his brother. Soon they emerged from the forest and struck the main trail that overlooked the village.

"Hey," Lino shouted. "Look at the houses from here. There's Lonco's Tavern, the one with the tile roof. Like you said, there'll be a tile boom in this village." He smiled as he teased his younger brother.

"Shut up," Augustine said. "Those roofs keep us in cash. If Lonco gets money from our drinking, we'll be poor as gophers."

Lino pretended he didn't hear. They plodded along the dirt road, then up a beaten trail that led into their village of Sayula. Gradually the raucous sound of the tavern jukebox reached their ears.

The music made Lino's eyes glint with joy. "Hey, Auguch, we're just about there."

Augustine strode on. "You're almost there. I'm going home."

As they neared the tavern, Augustine took one glance at the Friday afternoon crowd of men laughing and drinking, and then set his face toward home. He wished he hadn't looked. His older cousin, Chompa, sat chatting with friends near the open door as he leaned on a metal table covered with empty bottles.

Augustine and Lino were passing right in front of the tavern when Chompa's sharp voice stopped them.

"Hey, get on in here!" he ordered with the authority of an elder.

Lino laughed and hurried in, but Augustine headed on down the road. Chompa shot out of his chair, rushed into the street and grabbed Augustine by the arm.

Augustine tensed under the firm grip of his elder cousin. Chompa stood five feet tall, his muscular arms bulging under a ragged denim shirt. His jeans reeked with liquor that stung Augustine's nostrils. He looked with obvious disgust into Chompa's stubborn face. He detested that look in Chompa's eyes that said, You better come in or else! How can I resist this mulehead? he wondered.

"Sorry, Chompa," he said. "I've got to get home. Haven't

seen my family in two days."

"Okay, okay," Chompa agreed. "You can go home, but first come join us."

Augustine's mind clouded and the dazzling sun whirled his thoughts. His body ached with fatigue but Chompa's powerful arm held tight. And behind the drunk man's happy face stood stern authority that demanded respect. Besides, all his friends were there. Maybe just one drink, Augustine thought. He soon found himself at the table in the bar.

Drunken men slouched in metal chairs and leaned against small tables that cluttered the room. The jukebox blasted out an ear-jarring tune on a scratchy record. And barkeeper Lonco leaned on the counter, which half-concealed shelves lined with liquor bottles.

"Another round of drinks," Chompa yelled. The barkeeper waddled over. Clearing away empty bottles, he made room for the drinks. Chompa gulped his rum as his friends joined him.

Lino sat with his arm along the back of the chair. His eyes twinkled when he noticed Augustine's untasted drink.

"Hey, Chompa," he remarked. "Auguch likes good stuff. He hasn't touched his drink. I told him the boss is buying."

The barkeeper butted in. "Your boss gave me twenty pesos. Chompa's already soaked up that much."

A scowl crossed Chompa's face. "You're a liar, Lonco. I saw him give you fifty pesos. Get some good stuff for my little cousin, Augustine."

Lonco glared at him, then he grinned. "You win, Chompa. I'll get the good stuff." Soon he lumbered back with two fancy bottles of liquor.

The happy smile returned to Chompa's face. "That's better," he said. "Don't try to fool me."

Lonco pulled up a chair and plunked himself down at the table. "Tell me, Chompa," he asked, "have you seen the Americanos yet?"

"Sure I have."

"Yesterday I dropped in on them and got them to teach me some English."

"Yeah? Did you learn anything?"

"No," Lonco said with a snicker. "Their speech sounds like

radio static. But guess what? They want to learn our Popoluca language."

Augustine, interested for the first time in their idle talk, jumped into the conversation. "Why do they want our language?"

"Forget it," Chompa snorted. "Probably just a new scheme." He threw back his head and laughed. "Now's the time to celebrate."

As the men waited for the day to cool, they continued to drink. Augustine shrugged and grabbed the fiery mixture that Lonco had prepared. At first the beverage burned his throat and he coughed. Then a warm feeling rose within him, erasing his good intentions to go right home. Time rushed on—until he heard his name being called.

He gazed out the door. The blurred image of an old lady wobbled before his eyes. She was standing in the street, her tiny body rigid with anger, and she was glaring at him.

"Auguch!" she cried. "You drinking? Bella wants to know where you are."

Confused by the liquor, Augustine yelled at her. "What do you care?"

Chompa broke in. "What's the matter, Auguch? You've never sassed your aunt Ogo-Locha before."

Two forces stirred inside the Indian youth. Deep love and respect for the woman who had raised him struggled to the surface. But a stronger force obeyed the male, liquor-fed crowd that scorned women. That force made him mock the stubby finger that pointed at him now.

"Your wife had to shop by herself," Ogo-Locha said, her voice dropping to a whine. "And she ran out of money."

"I told her never to leave the house," Augustine yelled. He rose from the table, his face contorted in irrational anger. "Tell her I'm going to whip her."

A hurt look came over the old lady's wrinkled face, her voice turning to anger. "I'm going now," she said. "Beware if you hurt her."

Chompa grabbed Augustine and shoved him back into his chair. "Don't get excited, Auguch. You're letting your liquor do the talking. So what if Bella went shopping? Your wife has to care for you, doesn't she? Or is she your stepsister?" The sly smile on his face revealed a perverse pleasure in chiding Augustine for marrying his stepsister.

The men in the bar roared at the remark. Augustine jumped up, his face flushed with anger. But he didn't dare let his friends know he was angry with Chompa. Chompa laughed harder as his young cousin charged toward the door. Men rose to block him, then drew back. Augustine was growing violent as the liquor churned in his head.

Chompa bounded to the door and stood in front of him. "What's the matter, Auguch? One drink and you want to fight everyone. Can't you drink like a man? Control yourself!"

"I told her never to leave the house," Augustine muttered. Bella would pay for Chompa's remark! Pushing Chompa aside, he rushed out the door and charged into the burning streets of Sayula. As he reeled and lurched along, waves of anger roared in his mind. "I'll teach her not to leave the house!" he bellowed.

By instinct he followed the uneven trail along the edge of a deep ravine. Several times he fell and nearly plunged into it headlong. But each time he fell, he scrambled to his feet and drove himself along the trail.

Fifty yards ahead of him, his aunt Ogo-Locha hurried along, her face black with disgust. Finally she turned into Augustine's yard where his young wife, Bella, slumped in a hammock outside the palm-thatched hut. Near the door of the hut Augustine's old father squatted on a stool, weaving a fan out of palm leaves.

Simon Roman was a small man and thin like the strands of palm he laced together. His fingers moved skillfully and his face took on an expression of serenity as the fan took shape. Serenity with the old ways. He chided his sons when they bought paper fans for the ladies. Worthless stuff, Simon always said. This palm fan comes from God's forest and it'll last for years.

Bella caressed baby Tacho as he nursed at her breast. Red ribbons interwoven in her braids graced a face that was plain but warm with love and contentment. She smiled and greeted Ogo-Locha as she rushed into the yard.

The old man looked up, startled. "Hello, sister-in-law," he said, "What's the hurry?"

"Hello, brother-in-law." Ogo-Locha, anxious to warn the family, hurried through the required greetings. Her sister had died long ago, leaving seven children, including Augustine. Through the years she had helped Simon raise the orphans. Even when Simon had married Bella's mother, Ogo-Locha had continued to help them.

"Hello, Ogo-Locha," the young woman said. "Have you seen Augustine?"

Ogo-Locha spat out the answer. "I saw him at Lonco's—drinking with Chompa. Bella, he's coming now—and he's mad. He didn't want you to leave the house."

Bella's dark eyes widened. "I have to get corn ground for his tortillas. What does he expect of me?"

"We'll take care of him," Ogo-Locha said. "Take the baby and hide."

"But where?"

"Hide anywhere. A neighbor's house—anywhere. But go!"

Overcome with fear, Bella clutched her baby and scurried out of the yard.

"Quick," Ogo-Locha said to Simon, "let's get behind a tree and see what he does."

They hurried over to a gnarled *cocuite* tree, admired by the people for its tough wood, and now a good hiding place. Simon vented his disgust. "Those sons of mine won't listen. We never drank like they do now. I scold them, but it doesn't do any good."

Ogo-Locha clutched his arm. "It's not your fault their heads are hard like this bonewood tree. But shush! Here he comes."

Augustine stumbled into the yard. He bumped into a clay water pot and knocked it over. The pot shattered, making water gush onto the ground. He stared at the shards, then looked around, dazed and puzzled.

"Where is everybody?" he mumbled. He searched the yard, stopped and glowered at his empty hut. The door hung open on rusty hinges.

"Bella!" he thundered. "I told you never to leave the house." He stalked through the door.

The crash and bang of chairs sounded from the hut, then a heavy thud. Ogo-Locha nudged the old man. "Quick, go see what he's doing."

Simon hurried over to the door, then ducked his head as a chair flew past. "Auguch," he cried. "Have you gone crazy?"

"Get out of here!" Augustine yelled. "My wife has left her house. I want everything out. This isn't a home anymore."

The old man started to rush in but suddenly he skidded in his tracks. Augustine was lifting a wooden trunk and struggling to throw it outside. Simon stared, horrified. The trunk held all their clothes and other valuables.

The trunk was too clumsy for an enraged drunk. It slipped out of Augustine's hands and banged against the door sill, shaking the mud walls. He lunged at the trunk and shoved it outside. With a satisfied look he watched it crash to the ground.

"There!" he screamed. "This isn't a home." His strength now super-human, he wrenched shelves from the walls and knocked over a two-pound sack of sugar, making it spray over the dirt floor.

Simon yelled to Ogo-Locha, "Get the police. He's tearing up the house." He could have saved his breath. Ogo-Locha, the matriarch of the Roman family, was already hurrying up the trail.

Two men, drawn by the screams, rushed into the yard. "You're just in time," Simon said. "Help me stop Auguch."

The men grappled with Augustine and flung him to the ground. "Hurry," Simon yelled, "get a rope and tie him down. We'll string him up like an iguana. That'll teach him."

Augustine screamed and kicked while the men tied his hands and feet. Even with the rope binding him, he refused to give in. He squirmed and rolled on the ground, his mouth spewing out a volley of curses and oaths.

"Give him the iguana treatment," Simon yelled. "That's what he deserves."

The men nodded and heaved Augustine onto his stomach, then tied another rope connecting the ropes on his hands and feet. They drew this rope tight, which pulled his legs up behind him, and left him squirming on his stomach.

Augustine writhed on the ground. "Why did you tie me down?" he yelled. "Untie me! I'll tear this place to pieces."

"You're a stupid iguana," Simon spat out. "Strung up like

an iguana we take to market. But who'd buy you? Tearing up your home like this! And your wife was waiting to see you."

Ogo-Locha charged into the yard. "The police are coming now," she said.

Simon spat on the ground near his prone son's face. "Fine. A night in jail is just what he needs."

CHAPTER 3

Rum is a Mocker

At four o'clock that Friday afternoon the stinging sun still scorched Sayula's empty streets. A few Popolucas ignored the sun's fury and strolled aimlessly along the main thoroughfare, while others slouched on the cement steps of the town hall.

The loungers, curious about the outside world, watched the stream of vehicles passing on the new highway. Screaming semi-trailers. Lumbering cargo trucks. Shiny cars. Old buses. Elegant travel trailers belonging to American tourists.

On a hot day even this spectacle bored the loungers and they shifted expectantly, hoping to see something better. The air seemed too hot and oppressive for things to remain quiet.

"Look!" they cried.

The group came to its feet and moved onto the street. At the far end of Sayula's main street another crowd had appeared, thronging the police as they dragged their prisoner along.

Augustine kicked the policeman who clutched him. His hands were bound behind his back but he struggled furiously, lunging at those who held him. Two more officers grappled with him, forcing him along to the town jail. Simon and Ogo-Locha joined the throng. "Auguch, do what they say," his father and aunt pleaded.

Somehow their words penetrated his mind and Augustine quit the struggle. He shuffled along with the police while the town people forgot the heat and joined the crowd. By the time they reached the town hall, excited Popolucas had filled the street. The loafers rushed ahead of the crowd and jammed themselves together on the steps.

"Untie me!" Augustine cried. "Will you jail me with my hands tied behind my back?"

The crowd jeered and mocked the policeman. "Let him loose! He can't hurt you. You afraid of a drunken Indian?"

The policeman pushed Augustine up the steps while the curious crowd drew closer. "Get back!" one officer yelled. While two of them held Augustine, three more policemen shoved the crowd back. Finally they thrust their prisoner onto the porch of the town hall.

A guard untied Augustine. "He won't get away now," he muttered with a curse. "He's sopping drunk." Another guard found Simon in the crowd and yelled, "Sorry, the office is closed. A night in jail for him."

"Just as well," Simon shouted back. "One night in jail will do him good."

Augustine stood at the top of the steps and his father's words amused him. He already felt good. Policemen no longer clutched him with their tight fingers. He rubbed his wrists where the rope had eaten into his flesh. After he surveyed the gawking crowd, he studied the railing that surrounded the porch.

Suddenly he lunged over the railing and broke into a mad run. He hurtled through the crowd of stunned onlookers and bounded down the street. The crowd rushed onto the steps, cheering as they watched him flee. The policemen, purple with rage, charged into the mob and forced themselves to the bottom of the steps. Pushing aside the clumsy loungers, they raced after the fugitive.

People scattered while the Popoluca youth dodged old ladies and vendors who blocked his path. He cursed the crowd, snarling with clenched teeth as people seemed to dart out of nowhere to get in his way.

Abruptly his strength left him. The brutal hours at the oven, the sleepless nights and the liquor had drained his energy. He stumbled and fell. Despair washed over him as the tight fingers clutched him again. Uniformed men swarmed around, sneering, mocking their prey.

The policemen returned to the town hall dragging Augustine with them, his hair disheveled, his face haggard and expressionless. His struggle over, he felt like going to sleep forever. The officers pushed his limp body along the street, pulled him up the steps, and dragged him into the jail cell.

"Don't let him loose," a policeman said. "Good thing he didn't get back home. He made a mess out of his house. Let's get him behind bars."

CHAPTER 4

Tamales and Bloodshot Eyes

Morning light filtered in through the barred door hole of the town jail and struggled to illuminate the cell. Augustine lay sprawled on the cement floor, his arms and legs numb.

He awoke shivering from the damp floor where he had passed the night. Dazed, his eyes searched the room. Slowly he realized where he was and jumbled thoughts pounded in his mind. What about my job? he wondered. All that hot work! Did I ever get home?

The sunlight brought some cheer into the cell. Augustine peered through the bars and glimpsed the town president, Don Juan, climbing the town-hall steps and striding toward his office. Two guards threw open the cell door and brought Augustine in before Sayula's highest official.

Don Juan carried his seventy years with dignity, and his white hair gave him an awesome look of authority. He frowned at the guards. "Lots of prisoners for me today after a wild Friday night?" He lit a cigar, then looked up at Augustine. "Well," he chuckled, "you caught a young one."

Augustine stood in the doorway, his hair disheveled, work trousers rumpled, shirt still unbuttoned. The sour taste of rum lingered in his mouth. Just two days earlier he had prided himself as a master craftsman, ready to help his people. Now he was one of the rabble—defeated, crushed, humiliated.

"Get into the room," the guard said. He gave the prisoner a gentle shove and withdrew. Don Juan motioned for Augustine to sit down. He obeyed without a word.

Don Juan puffed on his cigar and leaned back in the chair. He ignored the clutter of papers on the desk and cursed the moist weather. The heat had not let up during the night and beads of sweat already stood on his brow.

The door opened and Simon and Lino shuffled into the office. Augustine bowed his head to escape the stares of his father and brother. A policeman jerked the door shut and snapped the lock. The two Popoluca men stood like upright poles, their bodies tight with anxiety.

Don Juan fixed his gaze on the prisoner. Augustine met his cold brown eyes and shifted uneasily in his chair.

"You're Augustine Roman?"

"Yes, Don Juan."

"And you resisted arrest?"

"I don't know, sir."

"You don't know." Don Juan grinned. "Were you drunk?" He released a loud laugh as Augustine squirmed in his chair.

"Not thinking of escaping, are you?"

"No, Don Juan."

The town president smiled at him, a smile of steel, defying the prisoner to try anything. He turned his gaze to the relatives. "Who ordered his arrest?"

"I did," Simon answered. "He was tearing up his house. He's my son, but I had to jail him."

Don Juan drew hard on his cigar and let the smoke swirl into his eyes. "This is a serious offense. Drunk conduct, rioting, resisting arrest. Well, fifty pesos fine."

The words struck Augustine like a blow on the head. A week's pay! he thought. He watched his father cringe. The old man looked like he had aged since Augustine had seen him a few days earlier.

"Don Juan," Simon exclaimed, "I had him arrested to teach him a lesson. But we are poor. I don't have fifty pesos."

Don Juan drummed his fingers on the desk. "Well, this is the first offense, isn't it? Thirty pesos."

"Yes, Don Juan. Thank you, sir. I can pay that."

Simon pulled a wrinkled twenty-peso bill from his shirt

pocket and frowned at his son, Lino. In turn, Lino withdrew his handkerchief and unwrapped a ten-peso bill. Don Juan kept drumming his fingers while they pieced together the fine.

"Just pay the treasurer on the way out," he said. He punched the bell on his desk and the door clicked open.

Augustine plodded down the town-hall steps, flanked by Simon and Lino. He trudged along the main street, too tired to return greetings from well-meaning passersby. Finally they arrived at the palm-thatched hut.

Bella and Ogo-Locha had already restored order to the tiny home. Now they were ladling tamale dough. They poured the soft dough into corn-husk wrappings and folded them up, then set them in a pot to steam all day. Hot coffee bubbled in a clay pot over an open fire. A gourd bowl containing hot tortillas rested on a table near the fire.

Dragging himself to the table, Augustine slumped into a chair. Bella set a steaming bowl of beans before him and hot coffee.

"There, Auguch, that'll make you feel better," she said gently, wanting him to know that she blamed the liquor, not him. "We'll have tamales tonight."

He snatched a tortilla out of the bowl and stuffed in into his mouth. When was the last time I ate? he wondered. This poor man's food tastes good.

He ate ravenously, then rose from the table and worked his way past the hammock where his son, baby Tacho, slept. Finding his cot propped up against the wall, he threw it down and fell into it like a sack of corn dropping to the floor. The meal dulled his mind and a stray breeze blowing softly into the hut soon put him fast asleep.

When he awoke, the room was dark and the rough voices of men rasped in his ear. The afternoon sun had already set and evening breezes cooled the night. Suddenly a familiar laugh jerked him wide awake.

"Chompa's come," he muttered. "Don't need an alarm clock when my cousin's around."

He searched the darkened room. Chompa and Simon were talking. The welcome bubble of tamales cooking in the clay pot soothed him. And over that sound came the pleasant tones of an old lady chatting softly.

"Grandma Mencha!" he cried. "You stayed away too long."

His grandmother turned her frail body toward him. "I've come, Augustine, my son. Let the tamales cook. Soon we eat.

The simple words cheered Augustine. So she's forgiven me, he thought. This is her first visit since the night I eloped with Bella.

The baby cried and Mencha scooped her great-grandson into her arms. Augustine smiled. He remembered a long time ago when she would give him a simple meal of tortillas, beans and coffee, while he sat naked on her dirt floor, his plate perched on a low stool. During cold spells she set hot embers beside him and the warmth made him realize someone cared.

Chompa grinned while Mencha cuddled the baby boy in her arms. A chuckle came, followed by a laugh. "Where did Bella pick up that foundling?" he needled, shaking with laughter at his own joke.

"The wind is rushing through your head, Chompa." Ogo-Locha's voice was angry but Chompa kept on laughing.

Augustine ignored his cruel humor. Joy overwhelmed him as he watched Mencha fondling his child.

"Look's just like Augustine," she said. "It's his father's son and my son, too."

The aroma of tamales made Augustine feel even better. How warm he felt in the acceptance of his family!

"Come to the table, you men," Bella said. "Time to celebrate Augustine's birthday. My husband is twenty years old today!"

Her words sent a shudder through Augustine. Can that be true? he said to himself. I started my twentieth year in the town jail!

Bella unwrapped the tamales and let them drop into a metal plate. The three men crowded around the table and began to eat.

Between mouthfuls Chompa asked, "Where's Lino and his brothers? Didn't you invite them?"

"Sure, we invited them," Ogo-Locha answered. "But they're out drinking. They got paid, you know."

A smile creased Chompa's weathered face. "Well, that's all right. All rumpots have to drink." He howled with laughter and Augustine nodded.

"They'll go ten days just drinking," Simon mused, a look of sorrow on his face. "How do they live without tortillas and coffee?"

"Ask Chompa." Augustine forced a grin and stared at his elder cousin. "He's the champion rumpot around here. He's a good teacher and his pupils learn quickly.

Chompa washed the tamale down with a quick swig of coffee. "We'll teach you yet, Auguch. You don't know how to ease fuel into your belly. You dump white gas on the fire and it explodes. You can't learn that way. But I'll teach you to drink like a man."

Anger simmered inside, but Augustine covered it with a smile. "Never mind, Chompa. I've got work to do on Monday."

"You'll work alone. The boss gave out too much booze. No one will show up except you."

Augustine sneered. "I always work by myself when the boss hires rumpots."

Bella stepped in between the two men with another stack of tamales. "Unwrap them and keep eating. It's time to be friendly."

"We are friendly," Chompa rejoined. "I'm helping your husband not to explode next time."

"Forget it," Augustine said. "I hope I never learn how to drink." He snatched up a tamale, forgetting his hand was sore from a burn received at the oven in the forest. The hot wrapping burned his hand and he dropped it. His untamed anger flared again. With a violent sweep of his hand, Augustine sent the tamale flying across the room.

He didn't wait for Chompa's hysterical horselaugh—or the indignant stares of the women. Jumping up from the table, he grabbed a bucket and headed for the door.

"I'm taking a bath," he said, "and then I'm getting out of here."

After stomping out to the three-walled stall that served as a bath house, he splashed water on his tired body. Chompa's laughter only made him scrub harder. Dressed in a clean white shirt and freshly ironed pants, he marched out of the yard, muttering, "How can I get away from that maniac?" It seemed he could never control his temper when Chompa was around.

The night air refreshed him. With brisk steps he climbed the path that led to Hidalgo Street. As he strolled along toward the town plaza, a familiar whistle beckoned him. The tone said, "Come here, old friend."

Augustine whistled in response, and climbed the knoll where his friend, Tino, was sitting. The glow from the streetlight revealed a handsome face that turned the heads of young women. What is Sayula's number-one ladies' man doing sitting on a hillside? Augustine wondered.

"Tino! How's everything?"

"Fine," Tino replied. "And how'd you like the town jail?"

"Don Juan snatched thirty pesos from my dad," he answered with a wry grin. "I'd rather consort with the real Don Juan of Sayula." Augustine smiled and poked fun at his friend. He remembered Tino's easy way with the ladies and how he once shocked the whole town by his amorous adventures.

"Tino, let's go find a dance somewhere." This was the first time he'd seen his best friend since Tino had returned from the city.

"Sorry, Auguch. You know that American family here? I'm studying the Bible tonight with Lencho the Americano."

Augustine's smile turned to a frown. "What do those outsiders want here? And what's this I've heard, that you believe like they do? Tell me it isn't true."

"It's true, Auguch." Tino glanced at his tile-roofed house that rested near the hillside. "Lencho is renting my house. I don't need it anymore. My marriage only lasted three months."

"What's the matter, Tino?" Augustine stared at his friend. "You, the champion lover? Now you can't keep a woman three months! You're slipping."

"She was no good, Auguch. I accused her of running around. We quarreled. Then her dad came and took her away. Now I'm back, sleeping in Mom's kitchen. But Lencho showed me that I needed to trust in Christ. I can't make it through life without God's help."

Augustine studied Tino's face, hoping for some sign that this was a joke. What made his old friend act differently? he wondered. He didn't talk like the Tino he once knew.

"Auguch, I'm a bachelor again. But this new way really helps me. Now I trust Christ and let him clean up my life. He gives me the discipline to live right."

Discipline! The word struck Augustine. His Mexican boss once said they could work at the factory if they disciplined themselves.

"Discipline? That word sounds good, Tino. We've always had a church here, but no discipline. The women gossip in church. They have processions through the street, then shoot off firecrackers and make a racket."

Tino's face lit up at Augustine's interest. "Hey, Auguch, come along to Lencho's house. They're learning our talk. And they want to write the Bible in our Popoluca language so we can understand it better."

But Augustine had his mind on something else. He looked along the street, now lit up by the beam from the electric light. He followed that gleam up the street toward the town plaza. His people never had electricity before. But the new highway opened the door for the convenience of streetlights—and made it easier for young men to carouse at night.

"No, Tino. The plaza is calling me. Too bad you won't come with me, like old times. I've got to stretch my legs. That jail cell was bad."

"Okay, Auguch. You know yourself best."

Augustine slid down the knoll and began his evening stroll up the street toward the plaza.

"I wonder what happened to Tino," he mused. "He used to be a real friend."

CHAPTER 5

The Owl Screams

At midnight that night Augustine sauntered along the street toward Ogo-Locha's hut. He appreciated his aunt, but her old beliefs and superstitions bothered him. She fussed about "bad winds" and the "evil eye", and she talked about witches. But she had a double cot at her hut, and since his own hut still needed repairs, he and his wife, Bella, had decided to put up with her old ways and live there temporarily.

Leaving the illuminated street, he turned onto the grassy trail that led to her hut. Once there, he crept into the dark room, trying not to awaken his wife or Ogo-Locha, who also slept in the one-room hut. After fumbling in the dark, he found the wide cot where Bella was sleeping and, flopping down beside her, he fell asleep.

Later, a nightmare disturbed him. He was riding a wild horse. It charged, reared, and tried to throw him. He clung to it while it bucked violently, and finally Augustine braced himself for a hard fall.

He awoke thrashing around on the cot, the pillow wrapped around his head. He expected Bella to scold him, but she kept on sleeping. For once he was glad his wife could sleep through a hurricane.

Ogo-Locha's quiet breathing came from the other side of the room. But sleep left him as cold sweat trickled down his back. He knew he'd be awake for a long time.

Suddenly he sensed something evil lurking in the room. A weird noise inside the hut reached his ears. He peered into the darkness and listened. At first he discerned only the dim outline of the rafters but gradually a strange fluttering sound unnerved him.

The form of a large bird was flying around inside the hut, back and forth above him. His mind half-numbed with sleep and fear, Augustine watched it. Then the thing dove straight at him.

He yanked up the bedsheet. When it swooped lower, he slapped the sheet on top of it and fumbled around to get hold of it. It was an owl—an evil omen!

Jumbled thoughts rushed through his mind. He belonged to a new age, but in the darkness of the Indian hut his mind raced back in time. Old people told of witch doctors who turned themselves into animals or birds. The owl meant witchcraft because it flew at night.

His reason struggled to take over. How absurd the old people! Owls enter huts to catch mice. But now the darkness and the mad fluttering under the sheet dominated his mind. Maybe an evil spirit lurks within this bird, he thought. I've got to kill it.

He clutched the owl and pounded on it. When it screeched, Augustine muttered between clenched teeth, "This owl's got to die." He hammered on it with his fist until it went limp. Is it dead? he wondered. Yet he couldn't release it. He beat it harder to make sure it was dead.

Worried, he searched out Ogo-Locha's sleeping form in the darkened room. Bella, dead tired from the day's work, had slept quietly through the racket, but Ogo-Locha stirred under her wool blanket. I don't dare wake her, he thought. She loses her head whenever an owl flies into the house.

His nerve left him and he called, "Ogo-Locha, wake up! I just killed an owl."

She jolted upright. "What!" she screamed. "Where is it?"

"Here in my bed. I caught it with the sheet."

Ogo-Locha scrambled out of bed and lit the kerosene lamp. The dull flame revealed her stocky old frame, clothed in the early-style Indian dress—square necked blouse and a faded wrap-around skirt. Her voice trembled with anxiety.

"Don't let it loose," she cried.

Augustine tried to chuckle. "It won't go anywhere. It's dead."

She rushed over, the lamp shaking in her hands. One look at the dead owl and her wrinkled face blanched with fear.

"Auguch! That isn't an owl. It's a witch in disguise."

He held back a smile. It was easier to be brave with the lantern and an old woman as company. "Don't worry, Ogo-Locha. I'll just throw it outside."

"No Auguch. It'll come back in. Someone sent a witch to hurt us. Cut it into pieces."

"Why?"

"You'll see, my child. You'll find a corncob or a piece of cloth inside it. Then you'll know it's a witch."

Hysteria began to grip the old lady and the thought nagged Augustine, Suppose she's right? It won't hurt to cut it open and set our minds at ease.

The old beliefs prevailed. He grabbed the owl and cut it open.

"Look, Ogo-Locha. It's a real owl. There's its heart, its liver, and all its insides." Smiling, Augustine looked up at her. His smile froze. Fear was etched in every line of her face.

"Auguch, witches are clever. Pour white gas on it and burn it up!"

His bewildered look made Ogo-Locha glare at him. "Auguch, you mustn't take chances with witch doctors. Burn it up, I say. Obey me!"

"But white gas is expensive. What's wrong with kerosene?"

"We can't waste time with witches. Stop talking and hurry."

He shrugged, took the owl outside, and poured white gas on it. "Hurry up!" the old woman urged. "Quick, take these matches."

A flash of flame lit up the night as the gas ignited. They watched the owl burn to charred remains. He hoped Ogo-Locha was satisfied, but her old face still tensed with anxiety.

"Auguch, get back inside! The witch'll come in if you leave the door open."

Augustine stared at her. He hoped it was all foolishness, yet how could he contradict his aunt? "Don't worry," he said, his voice full of triumph. "It's burned up. Now we can sleep in peace."

The old lady shook her head. "My child, at dawn you'll see I'm right. The owl won't be there in the morning.

"Ogo-Locha," Augustine said, trying to reason with her, "how do you know it was a witch?"

"Don't ever question me," Ogo-Locha replied, her voice firm. "I've seen strange things in my lifetime. Once the witch doctors tried to attack a woman who lived alone at a ranch. They turned themselves into jaguars. But she poured boiling hot water on the first jaguar to poke its head inside the hut.

"The next morning we saw this famous witch doctor. He was slinking around the village, and he had been burned—" Ogo-Locha's dark eyes flashed with fear—"burned with scalding hot water!"

Words left Augustine. He bolted the door and dropped on the cot. Ogo-Locha blew out the lamp with a quick puff. "Now the witches won't see us," she explained.

At dawn, Augustine stole out of the hut, the thought nagging him, Suppose the owl isn't there? Uneasiness gnawed at him as he looked around. Finally he found the burned remains and he sighed with relief.

But a fantasy leaped into his mind. The flash of light from the burning owl jarred his memory. Then the flame from the oven in the forest burst into his thoughts. Those fires spoke of two ages in conflict. The old age burned a harmless owl; the new age baked tiles to make better homes. He must belong to the new.

Staring at the black heap on the ground, he wondered, What can my aunt say now? A smirk curled his lip and he called, "Ogo-Locha! Come out here."

The thump of the cot banging against the wall reached his ears, followed by the sound of her quick steps. Jerking open the door, she rushed out, her eyes haunted.

She took one look at the charred remains and began to tremble. Gripping Augustine's arm, she cried, "Auguch, someone hates you. That owl came to tell you something. You must believe me, my child. Something terrible will happen to you."

CHAPTER 6

Scruples and Fears

Monday morning came without rain and the heat increased. Augustine strode to the village edge and climbed the trail that led to the forest. Trees closed in and shielded him from the sun, and the fresh earth on the path smelled good. Rounding a bend, he saw the majestic mango tree that marked the edge of the brick and tile factory.

Ugly jail cells and flaming owls swirled in Augustine's head. He hoped the boss would never find out that he spent a night in jail. He hurried onto the factory grounds and circled the work yard, his eyes alert for some sign of his boss.

A tall, stalwart man stood at the edge of a gully that bordered the yard. He hovered over Augustine's cousin, Chompa, and two other workers and angry words sputtered from his mouth as Augustine drew near. The Mexican boss turned and looked intently at him.

"Come here," he ordered. "I want you to look at something. See what you think it is."

"Yes, Don Nacho." Augustine watched uneasily. The boss picked up a bulky object that had lain half-buried in the ground.

The Indian youth took a quick look. "Sure, I know what it is," he said. "It's a stack of tiles. The oven heat welded them into one lump."

Don Nacho surveyed Augustine with approval, then

looked derisively at Chompa. "That's right," he said. "Careless workmen let the fire get too hot. I bet it was you, Chompa. I wonder how many ruined tiles you buried?"

Augustine stared at his cousin. The cocky smile melted from Chompa's face. Even though Chompa was probably guilty, Augustine hated the way the outsider bosses shamed his people into submission. Chompa assumed a fawning humility before his superior, bowing his head and speaking softly. "I don't know anything about it Don Nacho."

Don Nacho turned his gaze on Augustine. "What about you?"

"I don't know, sir," he replied. He continued proudly, "Last week we really sweated to do everything right."

The stony gaze of the boss softened. "That's what I like about you, Augustine. You've got the discipline for this job. From now on you're in charge."

Stunned, Augustine asked, "What about my brother, Lino?"

"I fired him. I looked for him last night and he was out drinking. These three men showed up. Get to work on those tile molds. I've got an order for six thousand."

"*Si*, Senor. We'll do our very best."

"Chompa," the boss said, "you work the main pit and dig hard. Remember, Augustine is the foreman. Do what he tells you."

Don Nacho whirled around, tossed the fused tiles into the gully and strode away, leaving Augustine staring after him. As he watched Don Nacho leave the work yard, he wondered, How can I boss my older cousin? And replace Lino? How unreal!

He rushed to the mixing area, the word "discipline" ringing in his ears. Can I say that in our Popoluca talk? he thought. Yes, we say, Don't do things without purpose!

Words he never thought he'd hear sounded in his ears as Don Nacho yelled at the helpers, "Get to work. Your boss has arrived."

He was talking about Augustine Roman. The one who had no schooling, who started out wrong in his marriage. The explosive one who landed in jail on his twentieth birthday! But he had a magic word—discipline. He would succeed!

Augustine and his crew plunged into the work. The boss gone, Chompa resumed his swagger and sauntered over to the pit. While shoveling the red dirt into metal cans, he clowned and joked, then rushed the cans to the mixing area. He treated the dead weight of the cans like a mere trifle. Back and forth he went, never tiring, never complaining.

Once he chuckled and exclaimed, "Ay, Chompa, work hard before Auguch explodes and kills all of us." His laughter rose to a high pitch as he hurried with his task.

The three helpers, dripping with sweat, filled the molds and rounded them firmly. Augustine worked like a dynamo, hurrying to and fro, finishing one tile, then running over to start another. The workers couldn't keep up with him. By evening he had finished a record two hundred tiles.

In one month Augustine and his men finished the 6,000 tiles. The young Popoluca surveyed the yard filled with stacks of tiles baked and ready for the boss. He grinned with satisfaction.

"God is big with us," he said. "We disciplined ourselves and did the job."

A few days later a swelling thunderhead threw a bright afternoon into darkness. Trails turned into rivers as drenching rain pounded the village. The rain shut down the factory for the six-month wet season. But Augustine, now bold with success and skilled at his work, boasted, "We can do anything we want. Hard work and discipline will put us ahead."

"Don't be so sure," his father, Simon said. The dry season over, he and Augustine sat together in their hut. Outside, the rain beat on the palm roof, and nearby tile roofs clattered under the hammering of a tropical storm. "You're always bragging, Auguch. Don't you know the "death month" is near and your Grandma Mencha is sick?"

Augustine shuddered. Every time he swelled up with confidence, his father would prick his balloon. "Why do you pay attention to superstition, Papa? Sure, she's sick, but she'll get well."

Simon shook his head. "August is the 'death month.' It brings dysentery and vomiting and kills its victims. That's what your grandma has. She may die, Auguch."

Augustine refused to believe his father. But as the month of August dragged to an end, old Mencha lay on her sickbed, burning with fever. While death lingered near, Augustine kept vigil by her side. Simon stood close by the sick woman, quiet, brooding. Outside, the afternoon thunderstorm added gloom to their thoughts.

A loud drunken cry tore through the downpour, pulling the two men to the window. Augustine's keen eye pierced the gloom and he recognized the alcoholic who stumbled along the street in the pounding rain.

"It's Chompa," he said. "On another drunk."

"Crazy fool," Simon muttered. "He'll sleep in the gully tonight."

They watched as Chompa struggled along the street, which had turned into a churning river of mud and water. He bellowed, cursed and howled like an animal.

A chill shot up Augustine's spine. Turning to his father, he asked, "Papa, what's the matter with all of us Popolucas? Rum grips us like a vine clinging to a tree."

"Don't know, Auguch." The old man sighed and stared into the storm. "It's just a part of us. You young folk drink more than we ever did."

"Not me." Augustine stood erect, his face set and determined.

Simon grinned scornfully. "What do you mean? I see you in the park with you friends, sopping it up."

"I just sip the stuff, Papa. I've got a new word. Discipline. My friends coax me to drink but I steel myself. That wild drinking in May cured me. Chompa's right. I'm explosive."

The old grandmother moaned and Simon returned to her side. Chompa's yelling grew fainter as the storm pounded on. Suppose someday I'll slosh in the rain like him? Augustine wondered. I made myself sound tough in front of Papa. But can I live any different from Chompa? Who knows?

Grandma Mencha died on a dark October afternoon. Mexican law demanded burial within twenty-four hours. By midnight a long pine table in the center of the hut held the coffin, hastily built of cedar wood. Bowls holding burning candles and incense surrounded the coffin, and underneath the table the family had spread lime in the form of a cross.

Eyes red with grief, Augustine and his five brothers sat

around the coffin. Relatives and friends who gathered for the wake had brought liquor to quench the sadness and stupefy the mind. His aching sorrow erased Augustine's memory of past resolves. Magic words no longer appealed to him. He began to drink. After all, he rationalized, everyone drinks in times of grief. And this time he didn't explode.

The next day the funeral procession wound its way toward the cemetery, and the Roman family, numb from liquor and lack of sleep, shambled along beside the coffin. Tears spilled to the ground as the men lowered the coffin into the open grave.

Augustine snatched up a handful of dirt and started to throw it into the grave. Suddenly a rough hand grabbed his shoulder and spun him around.

"Auguch, who do you think you are?" The voice belonged to his eldest brother, Lino, who glared into his face. "I get to throw in the dirt first. Just step back before I clobber you."

Anger flared, but before Augustine could strike out, his father's firm hand tugged at his arm. Simon stepped between them, speaking quietly. "He's right, Auguch. The older goes first."

Augustine shrugged and stepped away, letting Lino toss in the first handful of dirt. Then all the brothers scooped up dirt and threw it on the casket. The ritual over, the brothers stood at the graveside as the diggers shoveled in the dirt.

Looking away, Augustine noticed the Americanos in the cemetery. The blond one, Lencho, camera slung over his shoulder, stood with his fair-skinned American wife. Augustine nudged his father. Why are the outsiders here?" he asked softly.

"I asked them to take pictures of the burial," Simon answered. "Then we'll have something to remember your Grandma Mencha."

A bit if cheer crept into Augustine's heart. Maybe the foreigners weren't so bad. They respected the sad occasion and joined with them in their sorrow. And he would have pictures as a keepsake. He felt better.

Why are they living in our village? he wondered. Then he stopped thinking and stared vacantly at the grave. Later, the tiny group trudged home. Augustine stumbled into his hut, dropped on a cot, and fell asleep.

CHAPTER 7

What Shall it Profit a Man?

Firecrackers, gunshots and celebrations brought in the New Year. Old comrades embraced each other and drank together. The Roman clan celebrated and Augustine drank with them.

I can control myself, he said to himself. All it takes is discipline. As the banging rang in his ears, he looked ahead with confidence into the coming year.

At 3 a.m. Augustine found his Mexican boss at a table in the park. He chatted with him and finally warmed to the subject that pressed on his mind.

"Don Nacho, it hasn't rained for two weeks. When do we start making bricks and tiles?"

Don Nacho didn't answer. Instead, he leaned back in his chair and gazed at some revelers at the next table. Augustine thought he wasn't listening. "Sir, I'm ready to work anytime you say," he said.

The boss kept his gaze on the revelers and finally muttered, "They're fighting us, Augustine."

"I don't understand, sir."

"The cement workers." Don Nacho slammed his hand on the table and spat out the word "cement." "They're making tiles and bricks out of cement. No fire. No baking . . ."

Augustine struggled for words. "But . . . cement tiles crumble. Ours stay as hard as iron."

The boss shook his head. I'm shutting down the factory. Why fight 'em? I think I'll start my own cement works in some other town."

The words came as a numbing blow to Augustine's pride. As he strolled home he wondered, What can I do now? Only one answer: the cornfield. Go with his old father, Simon. Hack weeds all day under a hot sun. Return home with tick bites, skin torn by thistles. Plant corn with a dibble stick, poke holes in ground softened by rain, drop in a few kernels of corn. Drag home, exhausted.

Over the next month as he worked with his father, Augustine often thought of his old factory job. All those years wasted? Newer methods suddenly made his work obsolete. He could learn the new way. But not right now.

One evening Augustine stretched out in the hammock in his new one-room hut. His wife, Bella, put away the supper dishes, then squatted on a stool to nurse their new baby, Marta. Tacho, now a strong toddler, pulled an empty sardine can around the room and pretended he was steering a truck.

Augustine smiled as he watched his son. The hut was smaller than his old one on Ogo-Locha's land, but now they were by themselves. Bella had her cooking table on one side and the meal table stood on the other side. At night Augustine slung the hammock over a rafter beam to make room for their folding cot.

A familiar whistle cut through the night air. Augustine turned toward the open door and peered into the darkness. He whistled back, signaling his friend, Tino, to come in.

The kerosene lamp gave a yellowish glow and revealed Tino's handsome face and trim black hair as he entered. He took a stool and settled down near the hammock.

"How's your work, Auguch?"

"Fine. We keep busy."

"I hear you really make good tiles."

"That's all over, Tino." Augustine forced a smile. "Boss closed down the factory."

"Huh! I'm, sorry, Auguch. What now?"

"Cornfield. It's cooler out there."

Tino grinned. "That's where you buried all your money, isn't it?"

"He hasn't got any money," Bella broke in bitterly. "Too much dancing, too many friends."

"That really takes money," Tino observed. "I'm glad I'm through with that kind of life. But look what I've got!" He held in his hands a paperback book with a pink cover. "See what the Americanos have done! The Gospel of Mark in our own Popoluca language."

"What?" Augustine stared at him. "No one has ever written down our talk."

He took the book and opened it. Gazing at the letters, he thought, Is this my language? Slowly he sounded it out and read, "Here begins—the good news—of Jesus Christ—the Son of God."

He tried to read more but gave up. "Starts out all right. "It'll take work to unravel it."

"You can learn to read it," Tino said. "You became the champion brick and tile maker. You can do anything."

Bolstered by this bit of flattery, Augustine flipped through the pages and stared at the words that spoke his language.

"Lend me this copy. I want to study it."

Keep it," Tino said. "There are more at the Americano's house."

"Thanks, Tino. I'll tuck it away and read it on cold evenings." He smiled as he teased his friend, who knew full well there were few cold evenings in the tropics.

Tino accepted the joking with a gracious smile. "Listen, Auguch. I need a friend to help me walk with the Lord. We were pals before I trusted in Christ. Then we took different paths and that factory job kept you so busy we hardly ever saw each other. Maybe God stopped your work to make you think about Him."

Anger welled in Augustine's heart, but he held down his feelings. He prided himself on his craftsmanship. Such a comment from even a friend came like a slap in the face. "I don't know," he said. "Those believers seem happier than we are. But they slip and live wild like the rest of us. It puzzles me."

"We are all weak," Tino said, "unless we give everything to God. We fall because we move away from Him."

Slumped in his hammock, Augustine stared at the wall.

Tino waited for him to comment, then continued. "Let me read just one verse from this book. 'What good is it—if a man gains the whole world—and loses his life?' "

Augustine tried to ignore the verse but the message jabbed him. The hot toil under a blazing sun flashed across his memory. He thought of his painful labor at the oven. He had little to show for it. What had discipline done for him?

"I used to earn money just to toss it away," Tino continued. "But now I follow Christ. You know the temptations single men have here. But God has helped me to follow his trail for two years. It'll be easier for you. At least you have a wife."

Augustine kept his face blank, but Tino's words left him uneasy. "I'll study this little book," he said. "Our language looks good on paper. I had only three months of school, but I can read some Spanish. Now I'll conquer Popoluca."

"You can do it," Tino said as he rose to leave. "Think about it, Auguch. We stay together as a family. Now I need a Christian brother who will go with me. Come to the Bible study."

"Sure, Tino. I'll think about it."

He watched his friend disappear into the night. Disturbed by Tino's prodding, he looked at the pink book and leafed through it. Tacho toddled over to the hammock and slapped it. Augustine gathered him into his lap and kept on puzzling over the pages. His son grabbed at the book and Augustine pulled it out of his reach.

"Bella," he said, "take this book. Put it on the shelf before it gets ruined."

The Indian wife stopped her work, took the book, and placed it carefully out of reach on the top shelf.

But the pink book had stirred Augustine's curiosity. At the end of each day in the fields he lay in his hammock, mused about the field work, and wondered about the meaning of life. Questions crowded into his mind as he puzzled over the book called the Gospel of Mark.

The return of the wet season thrust Augustine and his father into long hours planting their fields. In the late afternoons Augustine bathed and put on his best clothes for his evening stroll. The cool breeze refreshed him and called him to another night at the plaza with friends and tapping his feet to the music of a dance band.

One night he crossed near Tino's house. Few homes had electric lights and the yellow gleam coming from the house nudged his curiosity. He drew near. Inside, Lencho the Americano sat with a cluster of young Popoluca men, huddled around a table. The men clutched booklets, trying to pronounce the Popoluca words on the page in front of them.

Slipping inside, Augustine squatted on a stool near the door. Light from a lone electric bulb shone down on the table, leaving the rest of the room in darkness. No one seemed to notice him. He crouched down in the shadows and tried to pay attention to the conversation at the table. Instead, a sore on his hand began to itch. As he scratched it, he recalled the thorny bush that had torn his hand just the day before while he was hacking away at some stubborn weeds.

Finally a voice penetrated his jumbled thoughts: "Is it my turn to read? All right. Verse 35. 'Jesus said: Whoever loses his life—because he loves me—he will save his life.' "

While these words intruded on Augustine's thoughts, he rubbed a scar on his arm. The old wound stirred another memory—the hot brick oven in the forest and the blazing ember that had shot out and seared his flesh. Now in the dark corner he winced as these impressions distracted him. Why can't I concentrate on what they're saying? he asked himself. He forced himself to listen as the next Popoluca read.

"My turn? Verse 36. 'What good—is it—if a man—gains the whole world—and loses his life?' "

The hot ember of God's Word seared Augustine's being. Where have I heard that before? he wondered. His mind raced to the evening he had slumped in a hammock and first listened to Tino. I once tried to gain everything, he thought. I've only got some scars to show for it.

The study ended. Augustine looked up, apprehensive lest anyone should see him. His rancor against these American outsiders still burned inside. But now his inner self impelled him to pay attention. Lencho invited the young men to pray. Augustine listened, questioning what it all meant. He recognized Tino's voice, praying. Then others prayed. They were asking God for his help and strength.

A strange urge to bow his head overcame him—and pray

along with them. No one noticed him. No one asked him to take part, but he wanted to pray. No words came, but he realized for the first time that Christ would meet his deepest needs.

The men at the table finished praying. Seeing them rise, Augustine sprang to the door and slipped out into the night. A few minutes earlier the park had tugged at his feet. Now his inner being pulled him back to his house. A smile spread over his face and he thought, Won't Bella be surprised to see me back so soon!

His wife gave him more than a surprised look when he strolled into the hut. He detected her angry glance when he reached for the pink book, the Gospel of Mark. When he stretched out in the hammock, the book open before him, scorn and contempt colored her words.

"Are you going to waste your time with that book?" she asked.

Augustine ignored the hostility in her voice and studied the strange marks that spelled out his language. Beyond those marks stood a message he needed.

CHAPTER 8

The Twisted Book

A violent August storm snuffed out streetlights and flooded roads and trails. Augustine stepped carefully along a mangled trail until finally he saw the white bar of light from the Americano's house. The glare from the gas lantern stood out in the dark night, inviting him in. He pushed through a crowd of children at the door, drawn like moths to a light, and entered the room.

Glancing around, Augustine saw wooden crates filled with books and papers, stacked against the wall. He noted the gas stove, the bottled water, the tape recorder. Why do they want so many things? he wondered. The strange habits of the Americanos intrigued him. And they were learning his Popoluca tongue! Few outsiders had ever attempted to unravel his complex language.

A group of young Popoluca men gathered around a cedar table with Lencho the Americano. Augustine felt more at ease when he saw Tino sitting with them.

"Welcome, Auguch," Tino said. "Come join us. Lots of room here at the table." Turning to Lencho, he said, "This is my friend, Augustine Roman."

He shook hands with Lencho and took a seat at the table next to Tino. Each student held a copy of the Gospel of Mark. Lencho offered Augustine a clean copy.

"We take turns reading the Spanish side," Lencho explained.

"Then we practice reading the Popoluca."

As Augustine studied the Spanish letters, vague memories drifted into his mind. Long ago an angry schoolteacher had pulled his ear while he stumbled through a reading book. How glad he was when his father, Simon, had pulled him out of school to work in the fields! Now at Lencho's house his turn came to read. He pronounced the words slowly, trying to get each syllable right. His self-confidence grew as he finished without making a mistake. The other students read until they had finished the passage.

"We read the Spanish because that's the national language," Lencho said. "But your own language is much more familiar to you. Who'll read it in Popoluca?"

"I'll try," Tino replied.

Augustine listened, amazed as his friend pronounced the words. They combined to spell out a message from God.

The reading finished, Lencho explained in faltering Popoluca the meaning of the story. Augustine kept a straight face, but the words that stumbled out of Lencho's mouth amused him. Maybe Lencho has a thick tongue, he thought. No wonder the old people joke about foreigners and say they need to whittle down their tongues.

After the study Augustine stayed behind with Tino. Notebook open, Lencho jotted down the new Popoluca words he had learned that night. Augustine watched him print the words. How curious the outsiders were!

While Lencho talked, Augustine leafed through the little book of Mark and tried reading more passages. He struggled to keep the sneer off his face. Should he tell Lencho how the book was full of mistakes?

He could feel old Simon nudging him. Respect the outsiders. Go along with them, Auguch. Agree with them. They know more than we do. But Augustine snarled in his spirit, I can't, Pap. I can't bow to outsiders. Why pretend?

As the thoughts struggled in his mind, he glanced up. Lencho was looking at him. "Can you understand that book, Augustine?"

The Popoluca youth blushed and shifted his eyes away. His arrogance left him and he groped for words. Finally he said, "Some parts of it are twisted."

"Twisted?" Lencho looked puzzled.

The color rose in Augustine's face. "I mean, some places are not clear."

"That's what I want to know," Lencho said. "We printed this first book to try it out, to see if Popolucas could understand it."

"We helped Lencho translate this book," Tino explained. "But sometimes we got sleepy and our brains went sour. We probably let the wrong things slip in."

And you were too polite to correct the outsider, Augustine said to himself. Tino with the easy tongue, quick to flatter the ladies to get in good with them. He did the same with outsiders, kindhearted, never offensive. You're a nice guy, Augustine thought, but you can't help people by agreeing with them.

Ignoring the interruption, Lencho asked Augustine, "Where is the book twisted?"

"There are lots of wrong words." Augustine leafed through the book until he found the page that had disturbed him when he had read it at home in his hammock. "Here's one right here." He jabbed his finger at the verse, expecting the Americano to get angry. Instead, Lencho smiled, found the place in his own copy, and read the verse.

"Mark 16:8? 'The women fled from the tomb. They trembled and were frightened.' What's wrong with that?" Lencho asked.

"You used the wrong word for 'fright.' It means they got 'fright sickness.' Want me to tell you about it?"

When Lencho nodded eagerly, Augustine continued.

"Once a neighbor girl fell into a well. After they rescued her, she just lay around the house, lost interest in everything and stopped eating. Everyone said she had 'fright sickness.'

"Her parents called in my aunt Ogo-Locha. She's the best fright-curer around here. She burned incense near the girl's bed, floated incense in a bowl of rum, then opened the window to let the bad spirit out. After that, the girl got better."

Lencho sighed as the explanation sank in. "Then this verse in Mark says—"

"That the women in the tomb got fright sickness," Augustine broke in. "It makes you think they had to find a fright-curer to help them recover."

A surge of relief swept over Augustine when Lencho grinned. But his next comment jolted him.

"Augustine, will you help me translate the New Testament? Right now I feel like someone out in the dark. I need someone who'll tell me when the translation doesn't speak good Popoluca."

Augustine stared at the floor. Finally he looked up, his mind whirling with doubts. Feelings against outsiders still embittered him. "I don't have time," he said lamely. "The cornfield takes up my days."

"You could study here at night," Tino said.

"That's right," Lencho agreed. "A few hours at night would make the Gospel of Mark easier to understand for everyone."

"Maybe I could come in the evening."

"Fine! We could read Mark and untwist it, make it talk straight."

"It needs it." Augustine broke off the conversation and listened intently. Raindrops sounded on the tile roof, signaling another rainstorm. The two friends jumped up, said a hasty good-bye and dashed out the door.

Once outside and safe on the next-door porch, Tino sighed with relief as the rain slowed to a quiet patter. He gripped Augustine's arm. "Hey, old pal, the rain's holding off. I've got something to ask you."

Augustine gave him an impatient wave with his hand. "Sure, Tino, but hurry up. Another five minutes and I'll get drenched."

"Listen, Auguch, Lencho has to leave next month. But I know a foreign lady who lives in Santiago City. She can really teach the Bible. Let's go to her classes and keep on learning while Lencho's gone."

"You keep hanging around outsiders," Augustine said with a frown. "Their Spanish talk darts around in your head like fleas on a saddle mat. Then you garble the Popoluca—and let Lencho learn the wrong words."

Tino flashed a smile at his friend. "I like your clear head, Auguch. Let's study the Bible together, even if it isn't in our own language. We can figure out how to say it in Popoluca. God's Word is our tortillas and coffee. When we load our heads full of the Bible, the devil can't scramble our thoughts."

Augustine shrugged. "Don't rush me, Tino. I don't even have time to study with Lencho. I'd better go now."

Heavy drops pelted the roof as Augustine hurried off the porch. But even though the rain persisted, he didn't run home. He plodded through the mud and clambered up the slippery limestone path toward his hut.

As the rain pounded on his back, the relentless words from Mark's Gospel beat into his spirit. "What good is it if a man has all there is in the world, and then loses his own life?" The verse drove into him and he kept wondering, Why can't I get those words out of my mind?

CHAPTER 9

God's Power Touch

A bright October moon illuminated Sayula village and lit the trail near Augustine's hut. In the distance a loudspeaker blared its invitation to an outdoor fandango in the town park. But Augustine turned his attention to the beauty of God's natural creation. Standing on the crest of a hill, he viewed the tropical trees. The moon flooded the forest and added a special charm to the night. His feet no longer tapped to the music. New thoughts filled his mind. Two years had passed since that first night at Lencho's and now he enjoyed evenings with Tino.

Tino should be along any minute, he thought. If he doesn't hurry, we'll be late for the Gospel meeting.

The loudspeaker sounded again and shattered the silence with the jagged notes of a Mexican jazz recording. Augustine felt caught in a struggle. He was learning more about God, but another force countered it. The songs of the world and its restless friends sought to win him back. But now God was conquering his heart. Maybe He could conquer Augustine's village, too.

Tino's whistle came through the night air. Augustine whistled back and soon Tino climbed the trail toward him. As Tino approached, Augustine mused over his struggle. Life as a believer is a new adventure, he thought. But how long can I hold out? He was glad Tino walked along with him and encouraged him.

They strolled along the trail until they struck the main road. Lencho's house was dark. Augustine wondered when the Americano would return from the States. Then he thought how he and Tino had contacted the foreign lady in Santiago City, interesting her in Sayula. She had asked Augustine to lead the songs at the nightly services which they held at Ogo-Juana's hut. But he couldn't understand why she continued to tolerate Chano as the pastor.

The foreign lady had wanted each town in the coastal region to have a pastor, and she agreed to pay him for preaching. Tino had suggested Chano, a native Popoluca who had been active in a local Christian sect before he had disobeyed the rules. Tino had said to Augustine, "Chano has trouble with rum like all the rest of us, but he knows the Bible. It's a shame if he doesn't use what he knows. Let's introduce him to the foreign lady."

Augustine recalled the night he and Tino had visited Chano for the first time in his tiny tar-roofed hut. He could still see Chano stretched out in his hammock, tall and thin with two missing front teeth and deep-set brown eyes, which gave him a hollow look. Tino told him about the foreign lady and how she wanted a pastor for Sayula.

"This is a hard region, Tino," Chano replied.

"We've got to struggle to keep on with the Lord," Tino said. "You've studied the Bible, right?"

"Sure, I know the Bible." Chano smiled with pride. "I know about the Jewish tabernacle, about the Urim and Thummim, the Levitical breastplate," he said, speaking the strange words in Spanish. "But the people here can't learn."

"You could teach them. The foreign lady wants us to meet every night. We'd learn plenty if we did that."

"I'll think about it," Chano said, stroking his chin. "But the people here don't know Spanish very well."

"You speak our Popoluca language," Augustine said. "Why not use it?"

Chano looked at him in dismay. "Our Indian dialect is too poor. How do you tell people about justification or sanctification, or about the Urim and Thummim in Popoluca? You have to use Spanish."

Undaunted, Augustine warmed to the discussion. "There's an Americano that rents here. He wants to put the Bible into our language. Maybe he can help us explain those words in Popoluca."

"I doubt it. Our dialect doesn't have enough words. How do you say redemption or salvation in Popoluca? You can't. You've got to use Spanish." Chano sat up in his hammock, his face serious as he considered Tino's invitation. "All right, Tino, I'll come. You new believers need somebody mature and well-learned. I might get interested in teaching those Bible classes."

When they left Chano's hut, Augustine asked his friend, "What does he mean by Urim and Thummim?"

Tino broke out in a loud laugh. "I don't know. But don't worry. He likes to use those big words." But as the months passed, Augustine remained unconvinced that the undisciplined Chano, even with his big words, was the right pastor for them.

Now as the two Popoluca men drew near the town square, they saw the jostling crowd of people in the park. The loudspeaker hung overhead and drowned out conversation. Augustine stopped and watched some couples dancing to the rhythm of the music. This had once been his favorite way to spend an evening. He noted how the people crowded into the square, at least two hundred of them, some watching and chatting, others drinking and joking. Then he thought of the handful of believers who would come to the Gospel meeting.

"Wow, Tino. I remember when once the park drew me like a magnet."

"Forget it, Auguch. We've got something to live for and real joy."

They continued along the street and finally swung off on a trail that led to Ogo-Juana's hut. She was a no-nonsense older Popoluca woman whose zeal for Christ was stronger than almost anyone in Sayula. Soon the crisp chords of a wire-stringed guitar struck their ears, and they heard singing, with hands clapping to the music.

"Listen," Tino said. "Skinny Chu-Odi is here with his guitar."

"I knew he'd come. He's like one of our family. I wonder if the Great Chano came."

"He's got to show up, Auguch. The foreign lady said a pastor has to be faithful."

"He wasn't here last night."

"He probably got delayed somewhere," Tino replied. "But look! Wherever there's a jar of honey, the flies gather."

Augustine followed Tino's glance. A group of idlers loitered around the door of Ogo-Juana's hut, grinning and jesting. They enjoyed mocking the few Christians. The two men pushed through the crowd of loafers and entered the hut.

"Let the Hallelujahs in," jeered one idler.

"Just ignore them, Auguch," Tino whispered. "They don't know what they're saying."

Only a few people fit into the room. Chu-Odi, a man almost as thin as the guitar he strummed, stood near the door, one foot on a stool, his fingers moving over the strings. Some older women sang and clapped their hands. And Ogo-Juana stood with them. A wiry lady, her old face lit up with joy as she sang the Gospel songs.

"Help me, Lord," Augustine prayed. The taunts of unbelievers angered him, but he couldn't expect things to go easily. He wondered, Where is Pastor Chano? Then Tino nudged him. "Get the people singing," he reminded.

Soon Augustine's clear voice rang through the hut, singing the same chorus over and over: "The Lord's people keep on rejoicing. The Lord's people . . ."

After twenty minutes of fervent singing, Augustine, his voice hoarse, sighed with relief when Chano sauntered into the room. "Chano," he said, "are you ready to preach?"

Chano grinned. "Sure, I've got something. Just sing a few more songs while I flip open my Bible."

Augustine forced himself to lead two more songs, but he resented Chano's casual and irresponsible way. He's just another lackey for outsiders, he thought angrily. The singing over, he slumped beside Tino, confused, weary in body and sick at heart, wondering how this tiny group could ever amount to anything.

The loudspeaker droned in the distance and reminded

Augustine of two superhuman forces in conflict. Those forces—the world and the Gospel— converged on him like two opposing river currents, each demanding his allegiance.

When Chano started his obscure message in fluent Spanish the Indian women began to chatter among themselves: "I washed clothes all day and my children got sick. . . . and it was so hot today I didn't get the tortillas ready in time for supper and. . . ."

"Bite your tongues," Ogo-Juana said in a loud whisper. "Pay attention." The women stopped their chatter and began staring out the window. They had no idea what Chano was teaching with his big Spanish words.

Chano's message, heavy in doctrine, fell on Augustine like a dark cloud. Am I in the right place? he said to himself. He glanced toward the door. A way to escape. Just leave. But the idlers blocked the door, their faces contorted in silly grins. Tino stood beside him. His friend's strong faith bolstered him and challenged him not to give up.

The service staggered to a close with Chano's final plea. "Let's come to the front of the room for prayer."

Augustine remembered what God had showed him earlier that evening—God's work in creation when he had viewed the forest flooded in the moonlight. He longed for God's power in his life. He had drunk from the world's cisterns, found them broken, with stagnant water. A yearning in his spirit drove him forward in that tiny hut, even as thirst had once driven him mad for water when he worked at the hot oven in the forest.

The mockers at the door jeered and their catcalls enraged Augustine. But this time the anger drove him to the Lord to receive strength. He knelt with the others. "Lord," he prayed, "for years I have been pulled to do evil things. I ask You to pull me once and for all to Yourself. I want to do your will."

The struggle within him reached a climax. As Augustine prayed, his spirit glowed with a new warmth. Songs floated in from the park over the loudspeaker. Can you get along without us? their tones suggested.

Why not? Augustine answered in his spirit. Tino has. Why not Augustine? I can experience the same divine power to conquer old habits.

Strength poured into his body and peace quieted his spirit. Once he had wasted his money. He would spend an evening in the park and squander a week's wage to impress others.

The Scripture came to him again: "What good is it if we gain the whole world and lose our own lives?"

"Lord, make me a genuine Christian," he prayed. "Quiet my heart. It wavers like a loose saddle. Give me your life in my spirit."

He rose from prayer knowing he had the strength to live this new life. He felt equipped to go out among his people, clothed in Christ, ready to grapple with each situation that came against him.

Augustine and Tino said farewell to the few faithful ones in the hut and strode out into the moonlit night. Before long they emerged onto the main road and approached the town square.

More people had crowded into the park and the loudspeaker continued to blare its raucous music. The few immature believers at Ogo-Juana's hut kept exasperating Augustine. The tinny guitar, the singing, the women chatting and children crying. And yet they were the fortunate ones. They had found the one important ingredient in life as they learned about the Lord. Instead of the lure of the plaza, Augustine and Tino headed home for a good night's rest.

Augustine found Bella at home, busy with housework. Pulling up a chair, he took out the Gospel of Mark in Popoluca. "Listen to this, Bella. I'll read some so you'll understand God's message. 'Jesus said, You see those big houses. They'll fall down until not one stone is left upon another.' "

His Indian wife listened for a few minutes but suddenly the pride and defiance handed down from her ancestors surfaced. Though conquered by the Spaniards, her people still treasured their freedom. Now her husband's new path involved outsiders. Something within her rebelled—until she could discover some plausible reason for Augustine's actions. And husbands seldom understood that women's work is never done. Abruptly she turned her attention back to her work. She scurried around, dusted the chairs, and began putting away the dishes.

Anger began to thunder in Augustine's breast. I ought to beat my wife, he thought. Why are women so hardheaded? Then he remembered how Christ was conquering his heart. Lord, restore quietness to my spirit, he prayed. He turned to his wife. "Bella, you pay attention to this."

The proud look melted from her face and she obeyed her explosive husband. But she would show him that her work was important, too. Grabbing some corn, she squatted on a low stool and began shelling it while he read from the Gospel of Mark.

"'When you hear of wars, don't be afraid, for it is not yet the time for everything to end. One nation will fight another, and in many places there will be earthquakes, hunger and fear over the land.'"

Baby Marta interrupted with a loud wail and Bella jumped up. She grabbed the baby and began to nurse her. She laughed abruptly.

"Ay, Auguch," she said. "Only liars say the world is coming to an end. Why do you read such foolishness?"

CHAPTER 10

God Swings his Hammer

A January wind blew through the streets of Sayula and toward evening a misty rain set in. Augustine huddled in his chair at Lencho's house. Lencho had returned to the village to translate another New Testament book for the Popolucas. Now while the norther whipped the streets clean of people, sending them home to their cots and blankets, a quietness settled over the region. The village silent, the two men seized the chance to concentrate on translating the Acts of the Apostles.

Scenes from Acts tumbled around in Augustine's mind as he studied this book. Philip unlocks the Scriptures for an Ethiopian. Simon wants religion the easy way—he tries to buy the Holy Spirit. A blinding light from heaven hurls Saul to the ground. His life is transformed and he follows the same Christ he once persecuted.

My people don't know God's Word, Augustine thought. Our witch doctors consort with evil spirits. But God can change even hard people like Saul. What marvelous things He did long ago! What about today?

Suddenly he sat upright and listened. The rush of footsteps hurrying up the walk reached his ears. His aunt Ogo-Locha appeared in the doorway, her wrinkled face tight with fear. Still gasping for breath, she cried, "Auguch, come quickly. Nalo kicked his younger brother in the groin. He nearly killed him!"

Augustine rushed to the door. Excited Popolucas were running toward Ogo-Locha's hut, drawn by the groans and cries that rose from her home in the gully. Others, not willing to brave the slick limestone trail, clustered in doorways and watched.

Augustine and Lencho dashed down the trail, slipping and sliding all the way until they burst into the hut. Ogo-Locha's son, Boyo, writhed in pain on the crude bed. The youth fought for breath and struggled to rise while two men held him down. An old lady swabbed his forehead with alcohol.

Numbed by his own helplessness, Augustine stared at his cousin. His face twisted in agony, Boyo screamed as the sharp pain plunged through his body. Excited Popolucas crowded around the bed, chattering advice, making any words from Augustine useless. He thought about the older brother, Nalo. He and Nalo, first cousins, had grown up together. A friendly fellow, Nalo never hurt anyone—unless he got drunk.

Ogo-Locha hurried into the room and pushed her way through the crowd to reach her son. Then faces turned toward the doorway as a town policeman strode into the hut.

"We caught Nalo," he announced. "We locked him up in jail."

"Just what he needs," the old lady exclaimed. "Imagine two grown men fighting like they hated each other! Jail is just what Nalo deserves. Kicking his younger brother! Can you imagine it?"

Turning toward the door, Augustine motioned to Lencho to follow him out of the hut. They trudged up the pathway and stopped at the Americano's house.

"Does your aunt need your help?" Lencho asked. "We can study some other time."

"Nothing we can do," Augustine replied. "She has too much help already."

"Does Nalo really hate his younger brother?"

"Of course not. His mind flips into a rage whenever he's drunk. Too bad for Boyo. He just happened to be there when Nalo got mad."

"Hot tempers run in your family, don't they?"

Augustine nodded weakly. "Makes me think of Saul in the book of Acts. Anger drove him until Christ took him into his hand."

A knot of neighbors climbed the trail from Ogo-Locha's hut and Augustine listened to their chatter. "The brute! He should hear his brother scream. He deserves jail for the rest of his life!"

The world "jail" slammed into Augustine's mind. He recalled the time he had wrecked his own hut and terrorized his wife. He could still feel the policeman's tight grip when they had dragged him along the street. He would visit Nalo. But later. The town jail, the surly guards, his humiliation before the town president—all this was still too real for the Popoluca youth.

He plodded back to Lencho's house. Picking up the typed pages of Acts, he reviewed Saul's words to Jesus when he first believed: "What do you want me to do, Lord?" God transformed Saul. Before, he cursed believers; afterwards, he prayed to their Christ. Augustine thought of his own people. They also have to believe. This same Christ has the power to help them.

While January's cool days continued, the words of Christ flooded Augustine with waves of joy. He looked forward to evenings at Lencho's house. One evening they studied Acts Chapter 16. Lencho handed him the typed sheets of the chapter and Augustine went to work, checking the words, his mind alert to catch any errors.

Augustine relived the torment of jail as he read that chapter. Unbelieving men had thrown Paul and Silas in jail. Augustine dreaded the humid prison. But these were God's men. The Lord sent an earthquake and freed them.

He recalled how he had fled from the guards. But Paul and Silas didn't flee. Instead, they said to the jailer: "Believe in the Lord Jesus Christ, and you shall be saved, you and those at your house."

Those at your house? Your own family? Suddenly Augustine felt relief. Concern for his family rolled away as he placed their care into God's hands. He seized the promise of this verse and his anxiety melted. God would help his family to believe.

Night after night, Lencho and Augustine pored over the pages of Acts, making the ancient message speak in modern Popoluca. January drew to a close and finally the two men completed a draft of this book of Scripture, the first time ever in Augustine's Indian tongue.

One night, while he was giving it some finishing touches, footsteps sounded outside and he glanced up from his work. A band of Popoluca men framed the doorway. They were some of the believers who met at Ogo-Juana's hut.

"We're headed for Ogo-Locha's home," one said. Your cousin Nalo has a high fever and we're going to pray for him."

Nalo sick? Augustine wondered, Is God teaching him something? He hadn't seen his cousin since he had been jailed for his drunken fight with Boyo.

"Come along with us, Auguch. We'll encourage him to put his trust in the Lord."

Augustine and Lencho worked their way down the twisted path that led to the hut. A few weeks earlier they had charged along the same path to console Nalo's younger brother. This time no screams directed them. But in the same hut Nalo now lay on his cot, tossing and turning, his head burning with fever.

Entering the room, Augustine glanced around. Ogo-Locha hunched over her meal of tortillas and coffee. Boyo lay in a hammock, staring at the ceiling. Now recovered from his injury, he greeted the men lazily as they entered. The old lady rose from the table. Recognizing the believers, she shrank back into her chair. She mumbled a curt greeting as the Christians filed into the room but kept her eyes averted.

Those at your house, said the Scripture. Augustine sensed his aunt's deep hostility, but summoned his nerve and spoke to her.

"Hello, Ogo-Locha. You're having your supper?"

"You see I am, don't you?" came the sharp reply.

"We've come to pray for Nalo."

"Well, there he is." The old lady tossed her head toward her son's cot but refused to look at him. "You can pray if you want."

Augustine read her tone of voice that said, Let him suffer.

He deserves it. He shrugged and joined the believers who crowded around Nalo's cot. Looking at his cousin, memories of his boyhood friend came to mind, chubby Nalo, who once had fished and hunted with him. Now he lay on a sickbed, groaning under the burden of his fever.

After a friendly greeting, the Christians sang songs, read Scripture from a Spanish Bible, and prayed. Nalo's brain cleared briefly and he muttered, "Thank you. Someday I'll join you at the meetings." He moaned and turned over on the cot.

The believers started toward the door. "We're going now, Ogo-Locha," they said.

The aunt nodded, her eyes still averted. But in spite of her attitude, Augustine felt encouraged. One of his own kin had finally spoken kindly of the meetings. God was working, touching lives, correcting Nalo, showing his people a new way of life.

But even the forces of nature seemed to keep the Popolucas bound to their old life. Sayula warmed up like an oven as the months rolled by. Any effort beyond field work seemed not worth the bother. The scorching sun turned its angry face toward coastal villages, its heat driving men home early from the fields. Finally, they even forgot about work and turned their attention to the big May 15 festival. They had to honor their patron saint, San Isidro. They would feast and drink in honor of this saint who represented the working man.

The crushing heat gave Popoluca men more idle time to celebrate and the uproarious fiesta drove new Christians from their fellowship into the merrymaking. As Augustine watched them stumble, God's Word in his own tongue glowed within him. It poured strength into him to endure the heat of temptation. New believers needed the Word also. Augustine prayed for that day to come soon.

Weeks later, black storm clouds seemed to pour their loads of water on the sun, plunging day into night, and sending torrents of rain to hammer on tile roofs. Steaming mist rose in streets and fields. Sweat streamed down the faces of farmers as they began planting their fields.

"And your house!" The words sounded in Augustine's ears. He began to pray daily. "Lord, help my family."

Old Simon, slumped in his hammock, nodded politely when his son invited him to attend the believers' meeting. But he didn't go. "Long day ahead in the field tomorrow," he explained. "Need my rest."

Bella's reply came with harsh words. "I've got children to nurse and food to prepare. You men do as you please in the evening. When can I ever find time to go to a meeting?"

So each night Augustine left the house alone. And as he strolled along with his friend, Tino, he wondered, Can God really help my family to believe? They seem so hard.

Each night he came back from the meeting and watched his complacent family, busy with mundane tasks, shelling corn, winnowing rice. "These things have to be done," they said. But they were excuses.

One evening in August came too quietly for Augustine. The meeting over, he stayed up late with Simon, talking about their day's work in the cornfield. Fatigue dulled his mind as he pulled down his cot. But once in bed, sleep eluded him. The quiet breathing of his sleeping family annoyed him. Why couldn't he sleep, too?

He dozed, but each noise jerked him awake—the harsh bray of his burro outside the door, the cicadas drumming in the forest. Just as he dropped off to sleep his restless spirit warned him that the dark night held no good.

At four in the morning Augustine opened his eyes in the dark. He wondered what bad dream haunted him. Nature had hushed its voice, the roosters had stopped crowing, the burro stomped restlessly on the ground.

Gradually Augustine began to feel the vibration. His cot rocked like a hammock as the earth beneath began to slip. The hut shook, dishes rattled, a sickening "crack!" sounded in the wall. He struggled to wake up, hoping the mad sensation would go away. But as he leaped out of his cot, the hut kept moving and shaking.

Bella's scream tore through the hut. "Auguch! It's an earthquake! The world's coming to an end."

Augustine was wide awake. "Quick, get out of the house," he yelled. Scooping up her two children, the Indian mother rushed out into the night. Augustine dashed from hut to hut, pounding on doors, yelling at sleeping neighbors, "Wake up and run!"

Soon the tremor stopped. In the early dawn light the huts stood intact. Augustine stopped to thank God for sparing them. Frightened Popolucas stood in clusters, talking excitedly about the jolt and the rude shaking of their cots.

As the day brightened, reports flowed in. God had swung his hammer elsewhere.

Jaltipan town—twenty miles away— destroyed! The ancient church there in ruins.

Acayucan town—just five miles away—the big church tumbled to the ground, many homes reduced to rubble.

The Popolucas chattered all day about the earthquake, talking about cracked walls and broken dishes. And they said over and over, "God is big with us."

That evening Augustine gathered his family around him. Bella sat motionless beside him, listening while Augustine said, "God spared us today. Let's go to the meeting and thank Him as a family."

Bella nodded, the rebellion drained from her face. But Simon, standing stolidly by the door, stared out into the night.

"Papa, come along with us," Augustine said, his voice soft but earnest.

When the old man shifted his gaze to the floor and kept silent, Augustine shrugged and headed out the door. Bella, holding baby Marta, followed, and Tacho ran to catch up with his father.

On reaching the street, Bella glanced around and grinned. "Look who's coming," she said.

Augustine looked back. Simon was trailing along behind, a shy smile on his face. The young Popoluca man stopped—and thanked God for the earthquake.

He thanked God also for the Acts of the Lord. Lencho the Americano had returned with a big green book, and its title read, The Acts of Christ's Sent Ones. Augustine chuckled as he read again his life verse in the new book. With an earthquake fresh in his mind, he related even better to the Philippian jailer who first heard the words, "and your house!"

God disturbed people long ago when Paul came to their towns. "These who unsettle people all over the world have come here also," they cried. As Augustine read these words, he realized that this message in Popoluca would unsettle his family and friends—and shake them.

The Good News also shook Augustine. He wasn't prepared when the Americano approached him with a new plan, a plan that would tear him away from the lush tropics of his homeland.

CHAPTER 11

From Jungle to Desert

Augustine took in the strange new landscape. Rugged terrain stretched out before him until barren mountains on the horizon obstructed his view. Waves of homesickness rolled over him. He longed for the green tropics with the mat of shrub and grass that covered the land near Sayula village. But he had promised Lencho he would come to Mitla so they could work without interruption on translating God's Word into Popoluca.

Thick dust lay in the street and covered his shoes as he strode into town. He looked around at this different Indian village. How strange the Zapotec way of life, how unusual their customs and dress! Soon the two-story adobe building where Lencho lived with his family loomed into view.

He recalled Lencho's words: "We can't translate very fast in Sayula. The heat, the interruptions, the noise—they all confuse us. Let's go to a quiet place where we can study."

But why here? Augustine wondered. It was different from anything he had ever known. As he pounded on the massive wooden door of the adobe building, he considered how sheltered the Zapotec people were. Everything is wide open where we live, he thought. No walls, no barriers. We're free to walk around and visit one another.

Lencho threw open the door and greeted him. "Hello, Augustine. Welcome to Mitla."

The Popoluca youth smiled, relieved that someone spoke his language in this strange place. "I've been wondering what's inside these big walls," he said.

"Well, come in and see for yourself. We have our rooms here, a place to eat, and your own private room. The nicest part is an office. No one will bother us there."

Once settled into his new quarters, Augustine took a look at Lencho's office. The trim concrete walls and the tiled floor gave a neat appearance to the study room. Bookcases lined the wall, all filled with study aids that would help give understanding to the Bible text.

At the translation table Augustine scanned a stack of pages typewritten in Popoluca entitled, The Paper That James Wrote. They would correct it and make it talk good Popoluca.

Over the next weeks, Lencho asked Augustine question after question.

"Auguch, what do Popolucas think about temptation? Do they blame God for that?"

"Everything good comes from God, they say. Bad things come from the devil."

"Auguch, God blames our own desires. The devil tempts us because we want to do bad. Let's talk about the things your people desire."

"Like what?"

"What does the Popoluca word 'joojt' mean?"

" 'Joojt' is our liver."

"I notice you use that word when you are happy."

"Yes, it means our liver is shining."

"Tell me more examples that use the word 'liver'."

Augustine thought a moment. "When we're sad, we say our liver hurts." He watched as the Americano scribbled down the word.

"Any more examples?"

"We say someone is soft-livered if he is generous."

Lencho chuckled. "I suppose hard-livered means he is stingy."

"No. If a man works all day without getting tired, he is hard-livered."

The Americano wrote down all these expressions. Then he scratched his head. "But what about temptation? How do we say that?"

A smile crossed Augustine's face. "Well, when a Popoluca young man has a sweetheart, she pulls at his liver."

"Hey, that's cute," Lencho said with a grin. "But suppose someone decides in his own liver to do wrong?"

"Then his liver begs for something bad."

"Wow!" Lencho exclaimed. "Then that's the way to express lust in your language. Now we can go ahead and translate some verses from James."

An hour later Augustine looked at a new and meaningful Popoluca version of James 1:13-15.

> When a man is tempted, he shouldn't say God is tempting him, because God can't be tempted by evil, and He doesn't tempt anyone. Each man is tempted when his liver begs him to do evil, and those evils pull at his liver. And when that evil remains with him, he permits sin to grow, and when sin grows big, then it will kill him.

Augustine nodded in approval. And his own liver shone brightly because muddy verses in Spanish were becoming sparkling clear water in Popoluca.

The days slipped by. Augustine labored on the translation with Lencho and when the pangs of homesickness struck, he eased the pain with more hard work. When they finished the letters of James and John, the Americano announced, "We'll make this into a booklet for your people. Let's work on the Gospel of John next."

Later, the two men struggled with the third chapter of John's Gospel. Lencho put down his pencil and ran his fingers through his hair.

"Auguch, verse three presents a problem. The Spanish says, 'He who is not born again cannot see the kingdom of God.' Jesus says we have to be born twice to enter where God rules. How would you say in Popoluca, 'I was born in 1935'?"

"I began to exist in 1935," Augustine replied.

Lencho gazed out the window, as he often did when he didn't understand the Popoluca. "Can't you talk about being born, as they do in Spanish?"

"No, we say someone begins to exist."

The translator turned his gaze on Augustine, his face

puzzled. "But it doesn't make sense to say, 'If a man does not exist again, he can't enter where God rules.' "

Now what do I say? Augustine wondered. Maybe Pastor Chano was right. Some things we can't say in our Indian language. He stared hard at the verse. "We already exist. We can't exist again. What does Jesus mean here?"

"God does something special for us when we first trust him," Lencho replied. "An example is your friend, Tino. He did wrong before he trusted in Jesus. Then God changed him and now he wants to serve the Lord. Isn't there some way we can talk about the changed life of a new believer?"

Augustine pondered the verse some more. "We can say that God makes us new." Relief swept through him when Lencho scribbled down this expression—until Lencho shook his head.

"That won't work. Jesus said these words to Nicodemus, who was a grown man. How would Nicodemus respond?"

" 'How can a man become new again if he is already an old man?' "

"That's it!" Lencho cried. "That's the right way to express the new birth. We must become new people before we can enter God's kingdom."

That evening Augustine thanked the Lord. "O God," he prayed, "thank You for helping me. Working at a desk tires my liver but You showed me something wonderful today. You can express your thoughts to us in our own language. Help me to translate the Scriptures so my Popoluca people will come to know about You and become new people."

The dry heat and crisp mornings at Mitla stimulated Augustine's mind. Without interruption he and Lencho could work all day at translation. He enjoyed evenings visiting with Lencho and his blond wife, Nancy. Their two children brought back memories of his own Tacho and Marta. He looked forward to his return home. But God's Word is making my liver shine, he said to himself. My people need that message, too.

Days rolled into weeks. In John Chapter 10 they talked about the true pastor. Augustine wondered out loud, "Why is a church leader called a pastor?" Lencho tried to explain.

"Auguch, do the Popoluca have sheep?"

"No."

"Have you ever seen a sheep?"

"Yes. Once someone brought two sheep to Sayula, but they died. Couldn't stand the tropics, I guess."

"You'll see flocks of sheep in these desert places," Lencho explained. "God compares us to sheep. That's not very flattering because sheep are stupid. They stray easily and the shepherd has to find them. A true pastor leads the church and cares about the people in his group, because they might wander off."

As they translated the passage from Scripture, Augustine realized how much Jesus cares for His people. He read from John 10:11, 12 in Popoluca.

> I am that good one who cares for the sheep, and the good sheep-tender gives his life for the sheep. But one who just works for money, he does not care for the sheep. . . . When he sees the wolf coming, he deserts the sheep and flees. And the wolf seizes them and scatters them.

He and Lencho wrestled with each word and phrase and translated them into clear Popoluca. A sense of awe seized Augustine as the marvels of John's Gospel unfolded before him. His time in the desert equaled a Bible course.

One truth from the Gospel stunned him with joy: Jesus held him firmly in his hand. As he returned to his hometown of Sayula, he sensed God's hand on his life. He was ready to share his faith in Christ with his people. And without shame! Tucked into his suitcase were copies of the translated messages from God.

He jumped off the bus at Sayula. The May festival was once again drawing near and tents and booths lining the main street were cluttered with tables and shelves jammed with liquor bottles waiting for thirsty Popolucas.

Augustine recalled how he used to drink during festival times. Now as he ambled down the street, a new power surged within him. Trials would come, but God's Word empowered him. Each trial would strengthen his faith. Evil might pull at his liver, but he determined to give himself to God and receive strength to help his brothers in Christ. With God's help, he could endure the temptations of any celebration.

CHAPTER 12

The Hireling Flees

New Year's Eve in Sayula. Exploding firecrackers left the air thick with smoke. From every barrio the blast of *cuetes* deafened bystanders and sent excited children rushing into the streets. In just four hours—at midnight—the village would sound like an artillery range welcoming in the New Year.

An old man hobbled along, clutching a bundle of rockets as long as swords. As Augustine strode along the main street with his family, six-year-old Tacho turned to watch the old man.

"Papa, may we watch the fireworks?"

Augustine shook his head. "Not this year, son. We're going to meet with other believers until midnight and start the New Year with the Lord."

They passed the town plaza, swung between rows of houses, and walked along until a mud-walled hut with red tarpaper roofing appeared. Augustine gazed with pride at their new chapel. The believers had struggled to erect a meeting house in Sayula. Finally Pastor Chano had offered a parcel of land next to his hut and the Christians gratefully accepted.

Augustine stepped into Chano's hut and found him lounging in a hammock while his wife cooked supper over a smoky fire.

"About time to start the service, isn't it, Chano?"

Chano yawned, then pulled himself up from the hammock. "Sure Auguch. Get them singing. I'll be along in a few minutes."

Augustine glanced at Chano's wife, who poked at the fire while shielding her eyes from the smoke. "Will the tamales be ready on time?"

"Sure," Chano answered. "Later on we'll have our own feast to celebrate New Year's."

Soon after Augustine stepped into the chapel, others came in and took their seats. Gradually the tiny room filled with thirty believers rejoicing in the Lord. They sang all evening until Chano finally sauntered in, giving a message and later calling for testimonies. One by one the Christians stood and recounted what God had done for them during the past year.

While Augustine waited to speak, his old father, Simon, rose to his feet. His tiny frame shook with emotion as he spoke.

"This year I've believed in the Lord because I saw what God has done for Augustine. He used to get drunk and beat his wife. Now he loves her and the children. I want to follow the Lord, too. God has shown me a better way.

"I never knew about God's Word. We had no school when I grew up. I only knew our Popoluca speech and I never learned how to make paper talk. How grateful I am that now I can listen to God's Word in my own language."

Augustine's liver shone with joy! The Lord's powerful Word was penetrating his family. From there it would spread into the whole village and bring help and comfort to his people. He rose to his feet.

"I want to thank God," he said. "The Lord has remade me. I once thought religion meant following an image around the town. But why? The people recited prayers, then blew off firecrackers and went home to bed. Now you hear the fireworks in the distance. But let that sound remind us that we believers place our trust in the living Christ.

"Now we can understand God's Word. When we believe his message, nothing else matters as much. People laugh at us but Christ helps us to endure the ridicule. Even our way of feasting is different. Tonight we'll eat together as the family of God."

Later, the tiny group of believers filed into Chano's house for the New Year's feast. Women served up delicious turkey immersed in brown *mole* sauce, with heaping bowls of rice and stacks of hot tortillas. Tall bottles of soft drinks replaced the customary liquor.

Suddenly the night exploded as firecrackers and rockets zoomed into the air. While children rushed to the door and gazed into the night, Augustine and his family stayed at their tables. Wild shouts sounded from the park, but Augustine smiled with relief. He was no longer part of that mob. The coming year would be different. Christ was changing his life and making him strong.

Cool days gave way to the hot season and in April the Americano showed Augustine a bundle of thin, blue booklets. The cover said simply: The Letters of James and John. Augustine picked it up and leafed through the pages. The dusty days at Mitla rushed back into his mind. He and Lencho had struggled over each word and phrase and now the translated Word of God was reaching his people bit by bit. They had to have it all in their own language!

Later that evening he approached Chano before the regular nightly service.

"Chano, suppose we preach tonight in Popoluca." Augustine's voice was polite but earnest. He sat on a wooden stool in the preacher's hut while Chano lounged in his hammock and munched on a fried tortilla. His Indian wife set a steaming mug of coffee beside the hammock and Chano sipped at it while he chatted with the young Popoluca man.

"So! The Americano thinks he knows Popoluca. Now *you* want to preach in Popoluca. Just think, Auguch, we men understand Spanish. Suppose the town president walked into our meeting. What would he think if we were jabbering away in our language?

"What's wrong with our language?" Augustine leaned forward on the stool. He tried to keep his voice even but the old anger simmered within his liver. "I've worked on translation and discovered that God's Word comes through clearer in our own speech. Our people don't understand the big words you use."

Chano gagged on his tortilla and took a quick swallow of coffee, clearing his throat. He looked askance at Augustine. "Looks like you're hooked on Popoluca. Well, I'll go along with you, Auguch. You can use your little blue book and say something in Popoluca. After all, some old ladies never learned the national language. But when you're finished, I'll take over and preach in Spanish."

"Everyone here needs to hear in his own language," Augustine said. "Maybe the women will stop chattering in the meetings if they can understand the message."

"All right," Chano said. "We'll give it a try. Go ahead tonight and preach in Popoluca. But I'll be there to straighten it out in Spanish."

That night the women gave up their gossiping and listened intently to the Gospel message in their own language. As Augustine spoke, he kept one eye on Chano, hoping the pastor would detect how much the people enjoyed their own language. But Chano drummed his fingers on his Bible and stared out the window.

I'll just trust the Lord, Augustine thought. Someday Chano will realize that our language has value.

As hot months came and went, Augustine received fresh strength from the Word translated into his own mother tongue. He could express in Popoluca the hard concepts of Scripture. Now even Popoluca old people could understand God's message in familiar words.

On a wet July day Augustine worked his way along a street washed out by hard rains. He walked by rows of palm-thatched huts and finally came to Beto's general store. Leaping the concrete steps two at a time, he strolled into the room.

Beto, Sayula's leading merchant, leaned on the counter, reading a blue booklet. His receding hairline made him look older and more learned than his thirty years. Augustine pulled up a chair to the counter and sat down. He smiled when he saw the booklet.

"Hi, Beto. Learning to read Popoluca? Where did you get it?"

"The Americano gave it to me." Beto flipped the booklet

onto the counter and looked at Augustine. "The letters are hard to figure out."

"It takes practice," Augustine said. "It gets easier as you work at it."

Beto narrowed his eyes and looked curiously at the young Popoluca. "What's the matter with you, Auguch? Ever since you got religion you don't come around and chat anymore."

"I'm busy, Beto. Field work during the day, meetings at night. Don't you like God's Word in Popoluca?"

A smirk lifted Beto's lip. "Look, Auguch. I remember when you used to talk sense. You wanted to help the people here. Who takes away their land? Outsiders, no? Now you're running around with them."

Augustine shifted uneasily in his chair. "God's Word will help all of us here live better."

"Forget it, man!" Beto slapped the counter and Augustine winced. "Do you know what my God is?"

Augustine shook his head, then watched in amazement as Beto pointed to the floor. "You mean the devil?" he asked incredulously.

"Try to understand," Beto said with a sly grin. "I don't believe in any religious nonsense. Not even the devil. What's important is the stuff this store rests on. Land, Auguch, land! Earth, dirt, soil. You walk on it every day. Yet those outsiders want to pull it out from under you."

Trying to control his temper, Augustine stood up and shoved the chair back in place. "Listen, Beto. I'm still interested in people. As long as the foreigners help us know about God, they are doing good. They don't want our land."

"They'll pull out on you, Auguch. Just when you need them. You don't believe it? Look at this newspaper!"

Beto gave a triumphant sneer, reached over and grabbed the daily newspaper from Santiago City. Thrusting it into Augustine's hands, he said, "Wait'll you read this!"

The front page looked like any newspaper and Augustine skimmed it until the lower section caught his attention. A photograph of a religious book stood out on the page. Its cover portrayed Christ blessing an old man who knelt at his feet. The bold headline read: Santiago City Seen From Afar.

The subtitle made fingers of ice crawl up his spine. It read:

"A religious magazine exhibits our city as truly backward."

Augustine glanced down the page until his eyes rested on her name—the foreign lady who sponsored Chano, who supported the Gospel work in Sayula. The paper was attacking her. He read on.

> We received by chance a copy of this magazine. This periodical pretends to preach the Gospel, but they portray the people of Santiago City as savages. We reproduce here a commentary by the editors of that magazine.
>
> 'Sister Jones informs us of her work in Santiago City. Most of the people there live in palm-roof huts. One fourth of the people wear their Indian costumes in the streets. One half of the people sleep on the floor, and most of the families live, sleep, eat and cook in just one room.'

Augustine read on, stunned. The editors in Santiago City fumed about the defamation of their town and upheld the diginity of their people. He felt the biting sarcasm of the editorial.

Throwing the paper on the counter, he said a hasty goodbye. Beto's words, muttered between clenched teeth, stung his ears as he turned to leave. "So long, old friend. Give me time and I'll pry you out of that religion. I'll find something worthwhile for you to do."

Augustine hurried up the street toward the chapel. A few minutes later he dashed into Chano's hut. "Where's Chano?" he demanded.

The Indian wife looked up from the baby she nursed. "He's gone to Santiago City. This is the day he teaches a class at the foreign lady's house."

Frustrated, Augustine whirled around and charged out of the hut. But his-steps slowed as he walked across the yard. Doubts troubled him and he thought, Tonight Chano will explain everything to us.

A thundershower drenched the village late that afternoon and only a few neighbors braved the rain to attend the meeting in the evening. Impatient, Augustine started the service without Chano. But joy left him. Why doesn't Chano come? he wondered. The song service over, Augustine preached a message and ended the service. Still no Chano.

Augustine dismissed the people and went to Chano's hut to wait. An hour crept by. Finally the steps of someone sloshing through the mud made the Indian wife perk up her ears. She was poking at coals of fire when Chano's lean body appeared in the doorway. He entered slowly, his face gaunt and haggard, his nonchalant manner gone.

Chano mumbled a greeting and slumped into the hammock. His wife stirred the coffee and poured out a cup for him.

"What happened, Chano?" Augustine asked.

The preacher stared at the flames that leaped from the fire. Finally he looked at Augustine. "Things are bad, Auguch. The foreign lady has to leave town. She and her family were packing when I left."

"But why?"

"A mob gathered outside her house. They shouted insults and demanded she get out. It didn't look good and she decided to leave."

"Then what happens to us?" Augustine was almost panicking.

Chano gazed again at the flame, then stared at the wall. "I don't know. What a blow from the devil! Things will collapse now. All of us pastors depend on her support. Who knows what will happen now?"

"Maybe the editors will apologize for the uproar."

"It's too late, Auguch." Chano slumped deeper into the hammock. "She's gone. Took all her belongings and left. Plans to leave the country. Auguch, we can't go on now."

"We can still meet. . . ."

Chano shook his head. "I'm locking up that meeting place. We're through."

CHAPTER 13

Picking up the Pieces

Sunday morning dawned with gloomy skies as the wet season dragged on and turned the trails into mire. Augustine lay in his hammock, holding an old Spanish Bible. This morning his family would not plod through the mud to morning church service. The chapel on Chano's land was locked tight, the newly-made benches shut up inside.

He leafed through the Bible until Psalm 69 lay open before him, the words matching his mood.

> Save me, O God!
> The waters have come into my soul.
> I sink in deep mire where there is no foothold.
> I have come into an abyss full of water,
> And the flood sweeps over me.
> I am weary of crying aloud,
> My throat is dry and sore.
> My eyes grow dim while I wait for my God.

Augustine gazed at the thatched roof that sheltered him. He mused on his four years as a Christian. Seven years earlier he had slaved at an angry furnace. He had wanted a tile roof house with a cement floor. Could this ever come true? Four years as a Christian, money not thrown away on liquor or women, but still little to show for it. He glanced back at the Bible.

I sink in deep mire where no foothold exists.

"What's wrong? he thought. I want to serve Christ. Now the foreign lady's gone, Chano is discouraged, the church door is closed. Can I give up now?

But the horror of jail loomed before him, the arrogant guards poking fun at him. He imagined he heard cousin Chompa yell in a drunken rage on a rainy night. How hopeless the drunkard's life.

A distant loudspeaker crooned a sentimental song. For a moment the sweet words appealed to him. Augustine thought of his old way of life. Friends would welcome him back to the bars. Drunkards would no longer mock him.

But the music stopped. In the silence that followed he remembered what Christ had done for him. Words of a Gospel song replaced the void left by empty dreams and unfulfilled ambitions: "Oh, what joy! Now I'm a Christian." He looked again at the Psalm.

Zeal for thy house has consumed me.
I am the talk of those who sit in the gate,
And drunkards make songs about me.
But as for me, my prayer is to thee, O Lord.
Rescue me from sinking in the mire.

In the solitude of his hut Augustine bowed his head and prayed. "O Lord make your Word come true: 'Believe in the Lord Jesus Christ and you shall be saved, and those who live in your house.' "

A shadow blocked the light and he looked up. His father, Simon, stood silhouetted in the doorway.

"Auguch, two men are coming. They look like outsiders."

"More city people, Papa? Don't we have enough trouble already?" Pulling himself out of the hammock, Augustine hurried to the door and looked down the trail.

Two portly men puffed in single file along the path and drew near his hut. The first man wore expensive black pants and the elegant *guayabera* shirt worn by Veracruz men. The second man, not familiar with the hot climate, had on a brown suit and tie and carried a felt hat in his hand. They exchanged greetings with Augustine and sat down in front of the hut. The first man spoke.

"So you're Augustine."

"*Si*, Senor."

"We've heard you are a Christian. My name is Piedad. We are members of the Mexican National Church. We serve the Lord in Santiago City, but we also start missions in small towns where there is no Gospel witness."

Sounds familiar, Augustine thought. He recalled his trips to Santiago City to learn the Bible from the foreign lady. She had talked about hiring pastors for small towns. Now the hirelings were gone. He could trust only Christ. But these men?

"That's fine," he said. A wave of cynicism swept over him and he parroted Chano's words. "But this is a hard region."

"It's hard everywhere," Piedad agreed, "when men refuse to trust Christ. We want to hold meetings here in Sayula." He motioned to the brown-suited man. "This gentleman is our pastor, newly arrvied from Mexico City. Nicholas, tell Augustine about the work."

Nicholas wiped his brow and tugged at his collar. "Our church wants to help these villages," he said. "We would like to send someone each Sunday to teach the believers."

"He would be like a pastor?" Augustine asked, trying to disguise the skepticism in his voice. The word still sounded phony to him. Christ was the true pastor. Hirelings work for money. Whom could he trust?

Nicholas shook his head. "We call them lay workers. A pastor has special training and oversees the work. The ones we send share God's message with those who haven't heard it. Where could we meet this afternoon?"

"Here? In Sayula?"

Yes, Augustine. We believe God wants to start a work here."

"That's fine. But I don't know where you can meet. My hut is too small."

"Then we'll find a place. Would you go visiting with us today? We'll find a home that will take us in for an afternoon service. Then we'll invite people to come."

Augustine mulled the question. He felt attached to the

believers who had met at Chano's little chapel. But now they were scattered sheep. Already that day his liver had pulled him back to his former life. If he stopped now, he would also go backwards in the Christian life. Would it hurt to accompany these men?

"All right," he said. "I'll go with you."

"Do you have any Scripture in your Indian language?"

"Three books."

"May I see them?"

He handed them to Nicholas and watched as the pastor leafed through the Book of Acts. He expected a look of derision to appear on the pastor's face. So many outsiders disdained Popoluca and called it the language of donkeys. Instead, a look of amazement crossed his face, an expression that showed genuine interest in Augustine's language. Finally he smiled and said, "The Popoluca is too hard for me. Read some of it."

Augustine opened to Acts 16:31, read the Popoluca words and repeated them in Spanish.

"That's wonderful," Nicholas cried. "Take that book along and read some in each home. Your people will understand their own language much better than Spanish."

Augustine felt a warm heat of pleasure surge inside him. How different this man was from Chano! Mexican schoolteachers had yanked on his ear whenever he spoke Popoluca in the classroom. They strongly disapproved of using Indian dialects, he remembered. His people would sit up and listen to God's Word in Popoluca if a Mexican recommended it.

"We'll start whenever you want," Augustine said. "Papa, come with us. We'll tell our neighbors all about the Word of the Lord."

Simon nodded in agreement and a big smile came over his face. "That's just what we should do Auguch. We can tell people in our language and then they'll listen."

"Sure, Papa. God hasn't forgotten us. He is big with us. Let's go."

Stuffing the Scripture books into a bag, Augustine threw it over his shoulder and headed down the trail with the two outsiders, and Simón ambled along behind them. They went from hut to hut greeting the people and read from the

Scriptures to them.

Once they came to a knoll and Augustine looked down at the hut that rested on the edge of the ravine. He nudged Simon. "We might as well bypass that hut. You know who lives there."

"Of course. Your aunt Ogo-Locha."

"Papa, would we dare say anything to her? She has no use for Christians."

"We've got to have faith, Auguch. The Lord wants everyone to hear his Word. Then the choice is up to them."

Rebuked by his father's quiet trust in Christ, Augustine bowed his head in prayer. The voice of God said, "Go, my child, in my name. I'll be with you."

"Let's go, Papa. God is able." Addressing the outsiders in Spanish, he said, "We'll visit my aunt next. But be careful. That trail is treacherous."

The men struggled down the slippery embankment and approached the small patio that surrounded the old lady's hut. Augustine went to the door and called, "Ogo-Locha! We've come to see you."

A thin voice answered from within. "That you, Auguch? Come in, my son."

"Two men are here with me. We'll sit outside."

They waited in the cool shade until Ogo-Locha appeared in the doorway. Her restless black eyes surveyed the two outsiders, her wrinkled face dark with suspicion.

"Ogo-Locha, these men preach God's Word. They want to tell you about the Lord."

She nodded but remained standing in the doorway. Augustine placed a chair near her. "Sit down, Ogo-Locha."

"I'll stand," she said.

Her cold attitude made him draw back. His people always put out chairs for visitors. Only rude or defiant people stood in the presence of company. But Augustine remembered God's voice and determined to make the best of an uneasy situation. Turning to the pastor, he said, "Do you want to read some Scripture?"

"I'll read from Acts 17," Nicholas said. "Then you read it in Popoluca."

As Nicholas read the Spanish, Ogo-Locha remained rigid

as ice. She stared at him, then her eyes darted to the other stranger Piedad. After studying him, she gazed at the ground. Nicholas finished and motioned to Augustine.

He read in a clear, loud voice, "God made the world and everything in it, and He rules heaven and earth."

Suddenly Ogo-Locha melted into the chair and began listening.

"He does not live in temples made by hands," Augustine continued. "We can't help God. He doesn't need anything because He gives life to everyone and He gives us air to breathe. He gives us everything."

'That's right, Auguch. God does everything for us." The voice came from Ogo-Locha, surprising him. Her face alert, she said, "He gives us our breath and everything else."

Augustine remembered her fear of "bad winds" and he thanked God. The Scripture was entering her liver. He read more.

"God made all people alike to live on all the land, and He gave the time and place for each man to live."

The eyes of the old lady began to glow as the full meaning of the Word came to her. "That's right. God gives us a place to live. We owe everything to Him."

Overjoyed at her response, Augustine said, "Listen to one more verse, Ogo-Locha. 'God did like that so people might seek Him, and if they seek after Him, they'll find God, because He is near all of us.' "

Augustine looked up at his aunt. The hostility drained from her face, she nodded in approval. "Those words sound good, my son."

"Those are God's words," he said. "He made everything. Once you scolded me for killing an owl; you thought it was a witch in disguise. But only God can make people, jaguars and owls. No man can turn himself into one of God's creations."

Ogo-Locha listened, her head nodding as she absorbed the truth of God's Word.

"I want my family to believe in Christ," Augustine said. "These men came to share God's truth with us. But we haven't found anyone who'll let us meet in his house."

"There's room here, Auguch, my son."

Surprised, Augustine exclaimed, "But Ogo-Locha, there's no room in your hut."

She shook her head. "See that hut over there?"

Augustine followed her gaze. "But that's Nalo's hut."

"He built a new shack out near his cornfield. His hut here is empty now.

Can this be? Augustine thought. Ogo-Locha helping believers. God's message in her own tongue has opened her understanding!

"That's wonderful," he exclaimed. "We'll invite everyone we see to a special Gospel meeting this afternoon."

And they did. At four o'clock the curious Popolucas crowded into Nalo's old hut. Augustine watched them file in and sit on borrowed benches, stools, even on old two-by-four lumber. To his amazement and joy, many of them were of his own family. They felt at home in a relative's house.

Three of his older brothers sauntered in and stood in the rear. Lino's tattered clothes reeked with rum after a seven-day binge. Anti, now the town broom merchant, and Pelto a farmer, stood with arms folded and listened to the Mexicans from Santiago City. But there they were, listening. What else could Augustine want!

Piedad, one of the Mexicans, taught them Gospel choruses and soon had the people singing. After he read Scripture in Spanish, Augustine read the same passage in the Popoluca speech. Later, the other Mexican, Nicholas, urged the group of humble Popoluca to take Christ into their lives.

The Popoluca men sat on the benches while others stood at the door, some stolid and impassive, others nodding in agreement. But God's Word pounded on their minds and tugged on their livers. Augustine thanked the Lord. In one day God had started a work in his family. They had all felt uncomfortable in Chano's chapel. He didn't belong to their family. In Nalo's old hut they felt at home.

Rainy days continued to gnaw at well-formed trails and turn them into quagmires. His people were like those trails, Augustine thought. Always changing, never firm. He puzzled over the handful of Christians in Sayula, each slow to grow in the Lord. Lazy in spiritual growth, they attended Gospel meetings, but later joined carousing friends and before dawn they were drunk. Would they always stumble?

Then he looked at his father, Simon. They were sitting together in their hut one evening while summer winds tore at the thatched roof overhead. The old man held his machete firmly on his knee and sharpened it until the blade glistened. A master craftsman, Simon demanded that his tool cut with precision.

"Keep shining it, Papa. Pretty soon you'll see your face in it."

Simon grinned. "Son, this machete is all I've got." Augustine leaned back in his chair. His father loved to spin the wisdom of his forefathers and Augustine enjoyed listening to the old man.

"One machete is all we ever needed," Simon continued. "This long knife hacked our weeds and harvested our corn. We used it to trim our palm thatch, to cut the poles and to dig postholes. It shaped our brooms and trimmed the edges to make them neat. We didn't need shovels and saws and woodplanes, like you young folk."

"You're right, Papa. Your fathers could teach us a lot of things. Your life was simple. But you never knew about the Bible. I thank God you now trust in Christ. I need you to help me when I get discouraged. The people are so slow to believe."

Simon put down his file and gazed at his son. "Augustine, don't look at others. You know what you have to do. God wants to use you like we use the long knife. He can use one tool for something good. Just trust him, Auguch. You don't have to answer for others, even if they desert you."

"You mean, like Chano and the foreign lady?"

The old man didn't answer. He picked up a broom pole and began notching the ends. Augustine knew his father. When he refused to answer, that meant the subject was terminated. So Augustine sat and mused on the words of Christ: "The hired one flees because he works only for his pay. I have come to give them life that continues on forever."

Why doubt God? He had to answer for himself and not for Chano or anyone else. Yes, it was worth it to be a Christian. He would continue to follow Christ, no matter what happened.

CHAPTER 14

Soda Pop is for Women

The coffee plantation surged with life. Children, grandmothers and aged men combed the hillsides looking for trees laden with the precious berries. Augustine stood on a knoll watching his family and friends pick the coffee trees.

The morning sun had climbed high into the sky and the stubby trees no longer offered shade. Augustine swabbed his brow and looked at the large can he had filled with the semiripe coffee berries. Then he turned his attention to a majestic cedar tree that rose high above other trees in the plantation. He gazed at the king of trees and noted its height and how thick its branches were.

We can get two rafter beams out of it, and at least eight cross pieces, Augustine thought. This time my dream will come true. No more palm-roof huts. If we sell our coffee before the price goes down, we can start on my new house. Stimulated by such thoughts, Augustine grabbed his palm bag and started in on a fresh tree loaded with berries.

One month later, the giant cedar tree crashed to the ground. The men erected a crude platform, cut beams and cross pieces from the red wood and then left the huge beams in the forest. Augustine's family united to build a house for him. They trekked to the forest armed with sturdy ropes and the strong muscles in their arms and legs.

Chompa swaggered along with them. With brute strength

he held up one giant beam while expert hands tied on the rope. All morning they tugged, pulled, and dragged the clumsy beam through tangles weeds and grass. Once in the clearing, they tied more ropes to the beam and hauled it to Augustine's yard. There the exhausted men gathered around an outdoor table, gulped rice soup, and stuffed pieces of tortillas into their mouths.

Chompa's eyes twinkled and he shook his head with pretended sorrow. Augustine understood the sign. He knew what his alcoholic cousin wanted. "Sorry, Chompa. No rum today. You need your strength."

"Bah!" Chompa snorted. "The 'cooked water' toughens us up. Give us rum and the next log will feel like a dry leaf."

The men, weary from work, nodded and ran their tongues over dry lips. They trudged back to the forest and stared glumly at the remaining beam. Suddenly Chompa let out a guffaw and yanked a rum bottle out of his ragged pocket. The men cheered as he passed the bottle around.

The next day they dug holes for the upright poles. Soon the skeleton of Augustine's home rose near his old palm thatch hut. His Popoluca neighbors helped carry 2,000 tiles into his yard and fitted them on the roof. Sixty men showed up to help. They brought in dry grass and began to mix mud plaster for the walls. But as the sun bore down on naked backs and sweat dripped off their brows, tempers rose.

"Give us rum and we'll work," they yelled.

The cry for rum increased and pounded in Augustine's ears. How could he violate the age-old volunteer work custom? A helping neighbor always expected payment in rum.

Lord, give me wisdom, he prayed. Suddenly a happy shout came from his father. Simon pointed at a truck that lumbered along the street, loaded with cases of soda pop. "Get some, Auguch. Thirsty men will drink that."

Amid cheers and shouts of derision Augustine stopped the truck and bought several cases. The men accepted it good-naturedly. But Chompa hauled out his rum bottle and his cronies helped him drink it. He cast an ugly glance at Augustine.

"We need muscle," he screamed. "Soda pop is for women."

The men laughed and kept on working. They dug a pit, mixed the loose dirt with water, and sprinkled in tufts of grass. Then they jumped into the pit and mixed the grass and dirt with bare feet. Old men carried wads of mud plaster to the house. They had formed a wall with bamboo poles and now they slapped on the mud and smoothed it down with quick fingers.

Augustine looked with pride at his new home. The roof gleamed with the cement tiles, the walls sturdy, the house large enough for him and his family. A verse from Proverbs stirred his memory: "The reproofs of discipline are the way of life."

"It looks good, Auguch." His friend, Tino, had strolled in and was looking with admiration at the new house. "I'm going to build my own home soon."

Augustine clapped him on the back. "Why? Don't you enjoy your single life?"

"That's all changed. Last night I eloped with my sweetheart."

"Well! You haven't lost your appeal to the ladies. Congratulations."

Tino blushed. "We'll get along fine. She's a Christian and wants to study the Bible with me."

"Where do you plan to build?"

Tino's answer came quickly. "Two miles from here, out near the highway."

"Why so far away, Tino? I like to have you nearby so we can talk about the Lord together."

"Auguch, I want to grow in the Christian life. Here the devil has something on every corner. The loudspeaker interrupts my prayers and Bible reading. Or someone invites me to have a drink. The women remember my past life and joke with me. Now that I've got a wife I want to live only for the Lord and start a Christian family."

"I know, Tino. But some of us need to stay here. We have to fight the devil in different places. When do you plan to build?"

"Before Easter," Tino replied. "I told the lay preacher from Santiago City about my plans. Right away he suggested a special service out there at my ranch."

"That sounds wonderful, Tino. Christians hold early

services all over the world on Easter morning. This time we can join them."

Two months later, the Christians of Sayula joined Tino and his bride at their new home on the edge of the forest. Easter Sunday dawned bright and clear. Children in the Roman family hurried along the highway, anxious to see Tino's ranch house. Older people waited for buses and some walked. Soon the small group gathered in the front yard. Carlos, the lay preacher from Santiago City, asked Augustine to start them singing.

Augustine rejoiced as he stood before his family. They were waiting to hear the Word of God. An occasional passing truck might interrupt the quiet, but the believers and others seeking the Lord were free from the noise and confusion of village life, ready to praise the Lord.

One family member was missing. Chompa had spurned the invitation. But Lash stood among the people who had gathered. Lash, the sixteen-year-old son of Chompa, was dressed in jeans and a denim shirt much like what his father wore. Augustine rejoiced to see Lash in the crowd. He thought, God has reached into Chompa's family and touched his boy. Maybe Chompa is too rum-soaked ever to believe. But with God working in Lash's heart, what more could we ask for?

Thirty people gathered, mostly from Augustine's clan, with just a handful from other families. But, he recalled, Andrew in the Bible brought his brother, Peter, to the Lord. And the Philippian jailer had won his whole family to the Lord.

Together they sang songs of Easter. The risen Christ was now with God in heaven and the little group of worshippers had much for which to thank God. "We have a living Savior," the lay preacher said. "The empty tomb is our hope. Other religious leaders are buried but we point to the empty tomb where they laid Jesus. He is not there. Our Lord is alive. He can help each one of us because He is with God and He is God."

Augustine drank in these words. His Sayula people made much of Good Friday and Glorious Saturday. But Easter Sunday was just another day to them. They didn't comprehend the resurrection. Someday they would also believe in this powerful Christ.

The morning worship came to an end and the group broke up and began their trek home. One person stayed behind. Lash, seated on a bench, looked intently at a copy of the Gospel of Mark.

"You really enjoy the Scriptures, don't you?" Augustine put his arm around his younger cousin and gave him a big hug.

Lash looked up from the page. "I really want to learn, Auguch. Every night I reach for some Scripture book and read aloud to my father."

"To your father? What does Chompa think of that?"

"I don't care what he thinks," Lash replied, his face set with determination. "The Bible can help us."

But doesn't your dad make any comment?"

"No. He just slouches in the hammock and listens."

"He never gets mad?" Augustine praised God that his stonehearted cousin Chompa was hearing God's message. "What do you read to him?"

"Those Bible stories you translated with Lencho the Americano. I read the story of the Prodigal Son, how he got hungry and envied what the pigs were eating. Pap just sits there and listens. Once I scolded him after he sobered up from a long drunk. 'You're just like the wayward son,' I told him. 'You live like a pig when you're drunk.' "

Augustine chuckled. "Did he get mad?"

"No, he just laughed. I don't talk about the Lord when he's drunk. He gets awful mad. Once he came at me with a machete. But he was too drunk to aim well. I had to rush out of there."

"Your father is a tough one," Augustine said. "Just keep telling him about the Lord. And invite him to the Bible studies at my house. He might come someday."

Augustine left Chompa in God's hand and labored with the Americano, Lencho, on more Scripture translation. They struggled with the hard theology of Paul's letter to young churches and found ways to express those truths in clear Popoluca. They plodded on until one happy day, two years later, Augustine and Lencho looked with awe at the Popoluca words: "May the Lord Jesus Christ give favor to all of you. Here it ends."

The words were not new. Many a Popoluca storyteller closed a timeless folktale with the expression, "Here it ends." But these words from Revelation 22.21 signaled the end of a huge task. Augustine and Lencho had translated the entire New Testament into the Popoluca tongue. And Christ had shown them favor. A few more years of revision and the New Testament would be ready for the people to read. And Augustine, his home now large enough, invited believers to study God's Word there.

Rain pelted the tile roof of Augustine's home. Inside, a tiny band of Christians crowded around a table. Augustine held his typewritten copy of Romans in Popoluca and explained God's message to them.

As the group talked about the Word of God, their hearts grew warm in spite of the cold night. Lash sat with them and told of his joy because he was learning more about God. Finally the study ended and the rain pattered gently on the roof. Lash got up to leave.

"I'd better run before it starts in again," he said.

"How's Chompa?" Augustine asked, still concerned about Lash's father.

"He's drinking again today."

"Drinking? He was showing some interest in God's Word."

"I'm still praying for him, Auguch. Who know's what'll happen to him?"

After Lash and the other Christians had gone out into the rainy night, Augustine closed up the house. He wrapped himself in a blanket and curled up in his cot. The village grew silent as fellow Popolucas snuggled down in the blankets to ward off the cold.

Sleep had almost come when suddenly a loud banging on the front door jolted him awake. Hearing Lash call, he jumped up and pulled open the door.

Lash rushed in, his face pallid with terror. "Auguch!" he cried. "Get over to my house while I go for the police. Pap is quarreling with Mama. Auguch, he's blind drunk and swinging his machete like a madman!"

CHAPTER 15

Five Pesos from the Devil

Augustine rushed along the dark path between the houses. Rain beat on the ground, but the cries from Chompa's hut urged him on. He slipped, caught himself, then forced himself on until he reached the ridge that overlooked Chompa's dilapidated mud hut.

Neighbors clustered nearby and chattered, but no one dared go in. Their self-righteous talk sounded in his ears as he headed for Chompa's door. "The brute! Beating his wife! Wait till the police come!"

Augustine worked his way down the slippery steps carved into the side of a hill. A scream pierced the night air and impelled him toward the termite-eaten door. From within angry voices shrieked and quarreled. Augustine pounded on the door until a child, his face frozen with fright, threw it open. He lunged into the room. Chompa, his machete uplifted, was ready to plunge the sharp blade into his wife's head.

"Stop, Chompa!" he yelled. Augustine wrenched the knife from him and flung it to the floor. He prayed for strength as he clutched his drunken cousin and forced him into a chair. Chompa lurched up but Augustine shoved him down and held him fast with a tight grip on his arm.

Chompa stared fiercely. Augustine shuddered before that wild gaze, the gaze of a trapped jaguar, a look full of hate and contempt.

"Get out of here!" Chompa screamed. Suddenly the wild look disappeared. Slowly he recognized Augustine and a savage grin came over his face.

"You've come, Auguch? I was ready to kill her. She's no good."

"You're no good, Chompa. When has your wife ever wronged you?"

The drunkard's words froze in his mouth and the wife, Macha, sucked up her courage. "Auguch, he threatened me with a machete," she said. "But it's his fault—been drinking all day. I've sent for the police."

"I'll get you!" Chompa yelled. Jerking up, he lunged at the woman. Augustine threw himself in front of the enraged drunk and grabbed his arm, holding him back. Chompa gave one last heave, almost knocking Augustine to the floor, when suddenly his strength vanished. He gave up the struggle and fell heavily on the bench. Chompa's thick body thudded against the wall, bringing down mud plaster on his rain-soaked clothes.

Jarred by the blow, Chompa's anger melted away and his haggard face held a look of amazement, then of frustration as he tried to regain his senses.

"Auguch," he muttered. "What happened?"

The thud of boots outside reached their ears. "Mama!" the child cried, "the police are coming."

"Let them come," Macha said. "He wanted to kill me."

"Don't you dare tell them that!" Augustine's voice was firm. "You know Chompa goes crazy when he's drunk."

The town police marched into the room and Lash followed behind them. They glanced at the drunken man who slumped against the mud wall, then looked at the wife for instructions.

Augustine spoke before she could accuse her husband. "He's drunk—been quarreling with his wife. He'll be all right in the morning." He stared at Macha and she understood his quiet plea. She stood silently, her body trembling, her face etched in fear and disgust.

Gathering around Chompa, the policemen pulled him to his feet. He shook his head in despair and resigned himself to go with them. Slowly the police led him out the door, past a milling throng of onlookers, and up the trail to the town jail.

Lash closed the door and barred it, and Augustine dropped into a hammock. Long ago he'd been in Chompa's sandals. Thoughts of jail brought back hateful memories.

"I'm glad I'm a new man in Christ," he said. "Macha, you did well. We want to help Chompa. One word about that machete and it goes harder against him."

"I thought Pap was getting better," Lash said with a deep sigh. "Now this."

"You can't give up," Augustine said. "God can help him to trust in Christ."

Hope flashed in Lash's eyes. "Auguch, I read God's Word every time he's sober. He was listening. I think he'll trust in Christ someday."

"Sure he will. And someday we'll get your mother excited about the Lord."

Macha blushed and stared at the floor. "I want him to forget drinking. He doesn't drink when he listens to the words from God."

"You're beginning to understand God's Word," Augustine said. "We have to give ourselves to God. When He enters our lives, we forget about bad things."

Macha nodded as his words sank into her. "Just this morning Chompa wanted to go to the believers' meeting. But someone told him about a ball game. I said, 'Well, go the ball game.' He left and never came back till now. He came home drunk and started a fight." Tears choked her words and she cried out between sobs, "I wish he'd gone to the Gospel meeting."

Augustine rose to leave. "Lash," he said, "you keep reading to him and make sure your mother listens. Tomorrow I'll go see Chompa."

As he trudged along the slippery path, he wondered when the Bible verse would come true: "Those who live at your house will be saved also." He thought of grizzled Chompa with his tattered jeans and ragged denim shirt. The disheveled hair and the wild look in his eye flashed in his mind and he shuddered. And yet God could help him. But when?

Morning came with overcast skies. Silence shrouded the town hall as Augustine climbed the concrete steps that led to the jail. Drawing near the heavy door, he peered through the barred hole. Darkness smothered the room and he could see nothing. All at once a hoarse voice rose from within the cell.

Augustine strained his ears to hear the faint words. A mumbling drunk? No, it was Chompa's voice—and he was praying! Excited, Augustine tried to understand the words of his prayer.

"O God," Chompa pleaded, "You see me in this place. O Lord, I've done wrong. Please forgive me. I want to enter in with You."

The sound died away, but the few words made Augustine's liver shine with joy. The dreaded Saul of Tarsus in the Bible came to mind. God had reassured Ananias with the words, "Look, he is praying." Why fear a praying man! Now Chompa's words, imploring God for mercy, filled Augustine with praise.

He peered into the dark room. Finally he discerned the bodies of drunken men lying prostrate on the floor. Chompa was among them, kneeling beside the wall. Augustine hated to disturb him, but he was too excited to wait.

"Chompa!" he whispered.

The dim form of his elder cousin rose from among the prisoners and soon his tired face appeared at the tiny window. "Augustine! You've come!"

"Yes. Are you all right?"

"Ay, Auguch. What went wrong? I woke up, thinking I was safe at home—until I ran my fingers over this cement floor. Right then God touched my heart. I didn't want to drink again, but the devil got me."

"You can't stop drinking in your own strength. God has to help you."

Chompa pushed his face against the barred hole in the cell. "He has helped me, Auguch. I asked Him to come into my life and change me."

"Are you sure?" Augustine had become numb to meaningless words from the lips of drunkards. A few days of remorse and then back to the bottle.

"Of course I'm sure. Have you ever heard me say I would stop drinking? You're hearing it for the first time. Believe me, Auguch. God has changed me."

Augustine returned home with lighter steps as he thought about God's work in his stubborn village. One by one the Popolucas would give their lives to Him when God touched them.

At ten the lawmen released Chompa. No one accused him—just another drunk to pay his ten-peso fine. A mild scolding from the judge and Chompa ambled into the street a free man. But instead of hitting the bars, he headed straight to Augustine's house and greeted his cousin.

The same wild appearance clung to Chompa, but now hope sparkled on his face. "Ay, Auguch," he said. "God taught me a lesson. Yesterday I went to the ball game. There I saw a five-peso bill on the ground. I pocketed it, saying to myself, God is good to me. I'll buy some sweet rolls for my children. Do you think I did?"

Augustine smiled. Knowing the ways of drunkards, he shook his head.

Chompa laughed at himself. Then his voice shook. "I got to drinking. They say I nearly killed my wife." He shuddered and grew serious. "I thought God gave me that five-peso bill. But no, the devil left it there. Just easy money to start drinking again. Today my family had to find ten pesos to pay the fine. And I missed my ride to work—a day's work lost!"

"It's worth it if you've entered in with God." Augustine put his arm around the man he once hated and hugged him. He was ready to forget the time Chompa had urged him to drink. He forgave the sharp words of abuse that had spewed from his mouth. "Chompa, you are my blood cousin. Now I receive you as my brother in Christ. If you've entered in with God, everything you've ever suffered is worth it."

Chompa nodded in agreement. "I have entered in, Auguch. I truly have."

Chompa with all his faults was a man of his word. He belonged to the older generation when no one learned to read or write. The spoken word was law. Chompa said he'd entered in with God and he meant it with his whole being.

Whenever Augustine opened his home for a Bible study, Chompa was there. When blustery winds or heavy rains held back the insincere or fainthearted, Chompa braved the weather and took his place at the table. Unable to read or write, he sat with head bent and took in God's Word as Augustine taught the Scriptures in Popoluca.

Once, when Augustine visited him, Chompa lounged in his hammock and chatted about his new-found happiness. Macha busied herself with tortillas, sent the children on errands, and set a plate of boiled bananas in front of Augustine. He decided it was time to talk to her.

"Macha, you hear Chompa talk about his new life. When are you going to follow him and enter in with Christ?"

The Popoluca woman evaded the question. "My husband doesn't drink anymore," she said. "He used to live with the pigs, crawl through the mud, then storm home and accuse me of things I hadn't done."

"Christ changed your husband," Augustine said. "As long as he stays near to God, you'll see a new man." He fell to eating the bananas. Between bites he queried Chompa.

"Tell me. What first made you think about following Christ?"

Chompa shifted to a new position in the hammock and began his story with eyes filled with awe at the mercy of God toward a sinner. "Macha is right. I lived like a pig. I made rum my water. I was married to liquor. I did anything for a free drink—help build houses, lug heavy rocks, anything. Once I even went with a witch doctor on his rounds. They demand liquor when they chant over their victims and I went along to help him drink the rum."

Here Chompa shook his head and chuckled grimly. He continued his story.

"Lash read God's Word to me. Ay, Auguch, I'm blind—I can't read. But my son wouldn't let me go in ignorance. I attended one of your meetings when that visiting preacher came. He said, 'Two young sisters were all dressed up and ready to go out, but their drunken father lay in the doorway. They had to step over him to get outside.' "

"God spoke to my heart. What did my own children think of me when I wallowed in the mud? But I couldn't change till I entered in with Christ. He gave me the strength to follow Him."

Augustine rose from the table. "Well, Chompa, God does strengthen us. Thank you, Macha. Time to go."

As Augustine rose from the table, he glanced back at Macha. She sat at the table, her head bent forward. She was deep in thought.

Augustine was thinking, too, but about the latest request from Lencho the Americano. "Come to Mexico City," Lencho had said. "Help me get the New Testament ready for printing."

CHAPTER 16

In the Soapmaker's House

Mexico City teemed with activity. Augustine jumped off the bus after his all-night ride from Sayula. Big trucks, speeding cars and giant buildings loomed before him, overwhelming him. He sensed how strange the brisk city was—droves of people rushing along with no time to talk, no greetings in the street, the rude throng pushing and shoving. But the time had come to help Lencho put the finishing touches on the New Testament.

Day by day Augustine worked at the Americano's home on the outskirts of the city. He checked hundreds of typewritten pages, all filled with Popoluca words, all declaring God's message in Augustine's own language. Later, they toiled over the final manuscript to make God's Word clear for the Popoluca people.

Before Augustine returned to his village, one thought nagged him. How could he help his people? Mexico City with its masses of people had a strange effect on him. The solitude of the forest came back to him, when long ago he had worked alone at the flaming furnace. Now he felt alone among the faceless mob that pushed its way along crowded streets.

A huge statue of Mexico's benefactor, Benito Juarez, stood alongside a park. Augustine read the words engraved on the monument: "Respect for the rights of others is peace."

Can that bring peace? he thought. His people didn't

understand land rights. Wealthy outsiders always exploited them. The Popoluca worked the rich land, but without title deeds anyone could snatch it from them—unless they knew their rights.

One day while mulling over the problems his people faced as they farmed their lands, Augustine strolled into a bookstore. He bought a small book entitled *Land Regulations* and, walking out onto the sidewalk, he thumbed through its pages.

Back home at Sayula, Augustine leafed through the land-regulation book. Gradually the truth shone into his mind like sunshine after a cloudburst. He could help his people get their rights. They didn't have to stay under the heel of the oppressor.

One afternoon while he relaxed in his hammock and studied the booklet, Beto, the town merchant, dropped in. He pulled up a chair and looked at Augustine's book.

"Still studying your Bible?" he asked.

Augustine ignored that taunt. "Beto, this little book tells how we can get ahead. We harvest corn just to sell it. During dry season we buy it back at high prices.The government can change all that. They'll help us build a grain-storage bin."

Beto surveyed Augustine with admiration. "You're right, Auguch. Our people need help. My father was a farmer; he hated outsiders who wanted his land."

"If only we could get the people here interested."

"They are interested. We should start a farmers' union."

Augustine sat up in his hammock. "Why don't we try it? We have to begin sometime."

"It's good to hear you talk sense, old friend." Beto smiled and took the book out of Augustine's hand and studied the cover. "Now this is the kind of Bible you need. Before you got religion, we used to be firends. After that, you didn't want to see us."

"I still trust in Christ," Augustine said, looking straight at the merchant. "But we should help our neighbors. Before I believed in Christ, I spent all my time carousing. I couldn't help anyone.

"All right, Auguch. No hard feelings. You're thinking straight. That's all I care." Beto gave the booklet back to Augustine and rose to leave. "Now you're studying the right book. I'm glad you're interested in land. We'll get together real soon."

Augustine watched Beto disappear around the corner of the house. Then his thoughts turned to the book he clutched in his hands. He chuckled while he thought, Beto called this my Bible. Well, maybe it is. It helps us solve land problems, just like God's Book helps us solve our spiritual problems. Suppose I help my people solve their problems. Later, they'll come to me with their spiritual needs. Then I'll help them find the way to God. Why don't I try it?

Each evening Augustine taught the few who showed up for Bible study. And using his new understanding of real estate, he and the believers bought land with an old tile-roofed hut on it. A little repair work and soon they had their own church building. And before long they would receive the New Testament in their own tongue.

He watched the struggling church grow. Chompa came with Macha, their children trailing behind them. Her liver now softened, Macha had trusted in the Lord and wanted to get baptized along with her family. Their son, Lash, now lived with his wife and children in a rude palm-thatch hut on the edge of their cornfield, a half-hour walk from the village.

But one humid afternoon in August, Macha rushed into Augustine's house. Gasping for breath, she cried, "Lash has quarreled with his wife. She's going to leave him."

Augustine jumped up from the table. "What! Where is he?"

He came in to tell us. Chompa is on the way out there now. Lash refuses to go back out.

"I'll go out there and talk with her. You come as soon as you can."

As Augustine bounded out of the house, the news burned into his brain like a hot coal. Lash and Rosa, both baptized Christians, were growing in the Lord. And Lash once had helped on the New Testament translation. He knew the Word of God. What had gone wrong?

Augustine ignored the black sticky mud on the trails. He hurried past cornfields, picking out grassy spots to walk on and crossing swollen streams on pole bridges. He rounded a bend in the trail to Lash's hut. All at once an infant's plaintive cry reached his ears. He rushed toward the yard, his hopes aroused. She's still here, he thought. Now he can patch any hard feelings.

He dashed into the yard—but no Rosa. Her frightened baby lay in a hammock, his wail now hoarse from crying. No mother consoled him. Rosa was gone, the yard deserted. In the dim afternoon light a gnarled hand pulled the hammock rope. Chompa sat half-concealed behind a crude door post, trying to rock the baby to sleep.

"Chompa, what happened?" Augustine cried.

His elder cousin rose slowly. The gaiety in his eyes had disappeared and he approached Augustine with heavy steps.

"Ay, Auguch. She's gone. Took one child and left the baby."

"Tell me what happened," Augustine demanded.

Chompa gazed at the empty yard. "You know as much as I do. I rushed out here and found everyone gone and the baby crying. What could I do? I got down on my knees and asked God for help. In the old days I would have got roaring drunk. But now I trust in God. I can't go the bad way again, no matter what happens."

"Thank God you stayed true to the Lord," Augustine said. "I don't know what's happening to the church here. But we've got to stand fast."

"But what woman would abandon her baby? She's no good, that Rosa. Why . . ." Chompa sputtered his rage, his anger rising. Augustine clutched his arm and gave him a friendly embrace.

"Don't get excited," he said. "My friend Tino once learned a proverb from an old Mexican rancher:

Estamos en la casa del jabonero;
El que no cae, resbala.

Do you know what that means?"

Chompa gave a hearty chuckle and the light returned to his eyes as he translated into his own language:

"We are in the soapmaker's house;
He who doesn't fall, slips.

The Christian life is a slippery path, Auguch."

"We ought to thank God He has kept us from slipping," Augustine said. "Let's get back and encourage Lash. Macha is coming along the trail now and she'll take care of the baby."

They found Lash at Chompa's hut, the sharp smell of rum on his breath as he ranted about his wife. "Well, let her go. What kind of woman deserts her home?"

"Tell me something," Augustine broke in. "Did you strike her?"

Lash evaded the question until the rum loosened his tongue. "All right, I hit her. She's been running around with another man. I struck her as hard as I could. Tomorrow I'll throw her in jail."

"It's too late, son." A look of pity came over Chompa's face as he broke the news. "She's gone. She took your older child and left the baby. Wc brought him home."

The news struck Lash like a sledgehammer blow. His face contorted and tears gushed from his eyes. Then anger welled and he cursed his wife. "May the devil carry her off!" he shouted.

"Try to listen, Lash," Augustine said. "We'll find Rosa and . . . ."

"I don't want to find her," Lash explained. "Let her go. If she comes back, I'll hit her again."

Augustine shrugged and started for the door. "We'll just trust in God now. Only He can work this out."

In the following days, Augustine thought often of the slippery path of a faltering church in Sayula. For thirty days Macha poured love and care on her tiny grandson. But even as she nursed the baby boy, her mother's heart warned her that he wasn't getting stonger. Finally life ebbed from the baby and one day Chompa broke the news to Lash.

"God took the baby. I sent for Auguch. Let him pray with us and read something from God's Book. When I needed God, you used to do that for me."

Lash buried himself deeper into the hammock. He stared at the wall, his face frozen in a bitter frown. "Forget it, Pap. My wife left me and deserted her child. And she was baptized! How can I face other believers? I'm not going to any more meetings."

Augustine called from outside the hut. While Chompa invited him in, Lash kept his eyes averted, staring into space.

"Read something from the Book," Chompa said, his eyes glistening with hope. "Something good for Lash. God can help him."

But even while Augustine talked and read from the Scriptures, he realized Lash was like a deaf man. He no longer heard. The deep sorrow in his liver had blotted out the Word of Life and it no longer penetrated his spirit.

That afternoon the burning problems of the infant church pounded into Augustine's mind. What is God doing? he wondered. Why can't I help Lash? Maybe it's time to help my people in another way. All at once Beto the merchant flashed into his brain and his acid words from long ago came rushing through his memory like a sour dream.

"Earth, dirt, soil. Land, Auguch, land! The stuff you walk on. Outsiders want to pull it out from under you."

"No, they won't!" Augustine cried out loud. Throwing on a shirt, he rushed outside and found the closest path to Beto's store. Soon the two men were chatting in a back room.

Augustine enjoyed the way Beto looked at him with pride. But he wasn't ready when Beto exclaimed, "I've got news for you, Auguch. People here want you for land commissioner."

Augustine stared at him, unable to answer.

"You're the only one who can do the job," Beto continued. "Now you can help your people. We meet Sunday morning to elect officers. Think it over, Auguch. Now's the time to act."

CHAPTER 17

"We Want Augustine!"

Augustine! Viva Augustine!" eager farmers shouted during their first farm-union meeting. "Augustine for land commissioner!"

The words from the excited Popoluca field-workers threw fresh hope into Augustine. At last an opportunity to really serve his people. The Sunday had dawned with blue skies, promising a special day, and Augustine felt fulfilled and happy. The three-hour meeting passed like a few minutes. The farmers voted on a slate of officers with Augustine at the helm. Together they would seek equal rights for land owners. And Augustine and Beto took a bold first step. They sent a petition to the governor, requesting a grain-storage bin for Sayula.

But the farm union threw Augustine into a whirl of activity as Popolucas came, their problems serious. Finally one night Augustine blew out the kerosene lamp and flopped onto his cot. Dead tired from the day's land squabbles, he welcomed the chance to sleep. The kitchen clock had both hands at midnight and the morning would bring still another man with more land problems. Sleep almost came when a soft voice sounded at the window.

"Auguch, you asleep?"

"Who's there?"

"It's me, Jose. Will you help me? They want to take away

my land."

He recognized the voice. Jose farmed a patch of land at the village edge. But why couldn't he wait till morning? Augustine wondered, exasperated. He dragged himself out of bed, struggled to relight the lamp, and then jerked open the door.

Jose entered and sat down. He held his thin body erect and shifted nervously, his dark piercing eyes checking the door for eavesdroppers. After he told Augustine his problem, he slipped out into the night.

Augustine returned to his cot, the responsibilities of his new office weighing on his mind. But he was determined to help his people, calm their fears, encourage them to struggle for their rights.

The next day he strode through the coffee plantation of two feuding neighbors, Chencho and Logio. Equipped with measuring instruments, they paced off the meters and set up stone landmarks. Beads of sweat gathered on Augustine's brow while they trudged into the humid forest of coffee trees. Finally they agreed on the boundaries. When they made plans to build a fence and settle past feuds, a feeling of triumph shot through the new land commissioner.

But that afternoon Logio slipped over to Augustine's house. He glanced around, made sure no one could overhear, then pulled some peso bills out of his pocket. "Listen," he said, "let's move that landmark over a few meters. Chencho won't know the difference."

Hot anger swelled inside Augustine and he fought to control his temper. "Don't you see, Logio? This farm co-op won't work if we don't do it right."

Disbelief spread over Logio's face. "I understand," he whispered. You're making it sound good."

"Get out of here!" Augustine yelled. "We're doing this farm program in the right way."

Logio's eyes turned into little slits of hate and he shoved the money back into his pocket. "Okay, Auguch. Do it your way. But you won't get ahead if you're dumb."

Augustine watched him rush out of the yard. The price of equal farm rights would not be easy. He realized more than ever how farm problems would squeeze him into a corner and force him to lose friends. He got up and headed for the meeting with his brothers is Christ.

Flies hummed in one corner of the believers' new meeting house. Outside a child rolled a noisy hoop down the trail while a sentimental ballad blared from a distant loudspeaker. With these sounds buzzing around, Augustine shook his head and tried to concentrate on the Sunday afternoon service.

To his left, Popoluca women and girls sat on rough straightbacked benches and watched the preacher. On his side, the men and boys shifted from time to time to more comfortable positions while they listened to a message from God's Word.

Augustine began to daydream. We have a church building on our own land, he thought. No one can snatch it away from us. And soon we'll have the New Testament in our hands. It's great to see men like Chompa here in the meeting, just beginning the Christian life. Gradually there will be more.

Sleep crept into his brain. He nodded and dreamed about last night's farm-union meeting. It had lasted until eleven o'clock while worried farmers told their problems.

Now he listened to the preacher—until sleep clouded his thoughts. It was easier to think about farm problems. They trespassed on Jorge's land. . . . They fenced off Jose's land. . . . They took a corner off Juan's cornfield. . . . They . . .

He heard his name called. "Augustine, will you close our meeting in prayer?"

As he prayed, he asked God to calm his mind and give him peace during the coming months.

Those months brought worries. One evening when Augustine hunched over a welcome supper of vegetable stew and tamales, he thought about his past six months as land commissioner. Worried farmers came at all hours, late at night, unexpectedly during dinner. Now he ate gratefully but quickly. He took big bites of his tortilla and chewed rapidly, hoping to get through before the next visitor came.

He looked at his family. Bella patted out tortillas while the children played in the corner. Tacho, now 13, sat at a table and studied his schoolwork. Augustine longed to spend at least one evening with them.

All at once he heard the sound he dreaded: the shuffle of

feet, an anxious voice outside calling his name.

Augustine jumped up, braced himself beside the kitchen door, and shook his head. Bella understood the signal and opened the door, leaving him hidden behind it. A man dressed in cotton pants and blue shirt stood outside.

"Is Auguch here?"

"No," Bella replied. "He won't be back until late tonight."

The man nodded, excused himself, and shuffled away.

Augustine returned to his supper. He hated officials who hid from people. Now he had joined their ranks. But he longed to see his family and have a chance to read the Bible. As he finished supper he wondered about the press of events that crowded him. And tomorrow night would bring the political convention in Acayucan town. He wondered if he would have the strength to go through with it.

Yet on Monday night he shared the excitement of the convention. Anxious delegates waited to see if their candidate would win the important seat in next year's senate. Augustine, Beto, and other farm-union officials joined in with the enthusiasm. The candidate they put forward had shown genuine interest in the farmers' problems and had promised to help the Sayula people.

The voting results came in, bringing from one section cheers and yells. But when Augustine and his group left the noisy hall, the cheer had gone from their midst. Their candidate had lost and now their struggle would be more intense.

The shadows left the empty streets gloomy and forlorn as they trudged along Acayucan's main street in silence. Some of them cursed and spoke of unfair elections and they moved faster to escape the din of the convention hall.

A cabaret flashed its neon sign in the distance and a lively tune sounded from a stereo. "Let's go in there," Beto said, winking at his companions. "We need something to cheer us up."

Augustine plodded along with them. Disappointment weighed him down. He thought, Why not join them? They had struggled beside him. Now in defeat he would stick with them.

CHAPTER 18

A Mirror for the Conscience

Augustine loaded the burro with dry firewood and headed back to Sayula. Nearing his home, he found Tino waiting in the patio. Untying the ropes, he let the wood crash to the ground, then he pulled up a chair and greeted his old friend.

Tino eyed the magnificent stack of firewood that reached to the eaves of the house.

"Getting ready for a big fiesta?"

Augustine smiled. "No. That's for the rainy season."

"It's good to be prepared. Are you ready for the big day?"

"What big day?"

"Dedication day is near. Lencho the Americano set the date for next month, on July 26th. The New Testament in our Sayula Popoluca language will be ready then."

Nudged by his conscience, Augustine thought, Ten hard years labor to see this day. And now village problems crush me like sugar cane in a press. "That's good news," he said to Tino.

"Listen, Auguch. They're planning a program in the town square. The town president and the judge will receive gift copies of the New Testament. They want you on hand to receive your special copy."

"Sure, Tino. That's great."

"We need someone from each Christian group to read from the Testament. Will you read a passage for our group?"

Augustine mulled over the idea. "Lencho asked me already. I told him I'm too busy. Why don't you read it?"

Disappointed, Tino looked away. Then he fixed his gaze on his friend. "You helped most on the translation and you're our best reader. The people think they can't learn to read their own language. If you all read it smoothly, they'll think differently."

What can I say, Augustine thought. He's right. But I've made enemies. Others criticize me for having farm-union meetings on Sunday. Finally he found a reply. "This land job takes all my time. You can read a passage."

Tino nodded. "All right, Auguch. But there's something else."

"What's that?" Augustine swallowed hard.

"The village gossips say you're getting careless. They talk about the way you miss the Gospel meetings."

"I have a tough job, Tino. I meet with high officials to get help for our farm problems. Sunday is often their only free day. I'm still trusting the Lord, but I can't refuse those who help us."

"God wants to help you, too." Tino's voice was soft as he pled with his friend. "Why don't you tell Him about your need?"

"My brain whirls like a spinning top." Augustine spun his fingers, imitating the wooden toy so popular among Indian children. "Everyone demands my time. People want help and they want it now. I can't put them off, like politicians do. I can't tell lies just to get rid of them. They trust me, Tino. How can I turn them down?"

"Whew!" Tino exclaimed. "You don't talk sense. "What's all that got to do with prayer? Even a spinning top comes to a stop and falls over. Why can't you stop and rest in the Lord?"

"I can't get close to God anymore," Augustine said, grimacing. "These interruptions keep nagging me and block out my prayers."

"Why don't you resign?"

"Not yet, Tino. This project means everything to me. Besides, the farmers wouldn't let me. I'll stick it out three more years. Once I get this program firmly in place, I'll get out for good."

"But you have to live for Christ."

Augustine shrugged as Tino's words pounded into his conscience. He said, "I intend to go on as a believer. And remember, Tino, Lencho and I sweated over that Testament. I look forward to the day when we present the New Testament to the people."

July 26 dawned with clear skies. A brilliant sun shone on Sayula village and a fresh breeze gave hope for a nice day. At noon Augustine strolled over to Lencho's home. Dedication day had finally arrived and Lencho's colleagues had come to celebrate the arrival of the New Testament.

Augustine greeted these friends. He had met many of them in bygone days when he helped Lencho with the translation. They all awaited the Bible Society director, who would bring the treasure—bound copies of the New Testament.

At 4:45 p.m. Augustine watched visitors gather around the kiosk in the town plaza. I've seen all kinds of events here, he thought. Orchestras up there in the kiosk, pounding out dance music. And politicians too, speaking from the same stand. Now my people will see and hear something different.

Lencho came along and interrupted his thoughts. "Auguch, are you ready? It's almost time to begin."

Augustine climbed the narrow steps inside the kiosk and emerged onto the platform. There he sat with the town president, the judge, and others in the program, and viewed the crowd below. About two hundred Popolucas stood in the shade of the platform to escape the sun's blazing heat.

At the stroke of five, the Bible Society director opened the program, followed by directors of the Mexico translation program. They spoke to the people and as Augustine listened, he thought with gratitude about these who had come from afar to give God's message to his people. He still hadn't seen a bound copy of the New Testament and he longed to hold one in his hands.

Lencho introduced the Popoluca men who would read from the New Testament. Lanu, a shy but handsome Popoluca, stood to his feet to represent one group of believers and he read in clear tones the message of John 6:25-35.

As he read, Augustine thought of Mitla town in the desert

where he and Lencho had toiled over this passage. The last verse caught his attention:

> Jesus told them, I am that food which gives life. He who comes with me will never be hungry. And he who believes in me, will never be thirsty.

He remembered how he and Lencho had worked out that verse. "Bread" meant only "Sweet rolls," a luxury item for the Popolucas. But Christ is real food for soul and spirit. The words inspired him to enjoy Christ more.

When Lanu sat down, Lencho said, "I've asked Rogelio to read from 1 Peter. Is he here?"

Some Popolucas in the crowd snickered and glanced at each other. Augustine felt the color rise in his face. That very day Rogelio, a local preacher in a splinter group, had given a wedding feast for his daughter and he had let her marry an unbeliever. He had struggled in the liquid world of rum before he started preaching God's Word. Augustine wondered if . . .

No response from Rogelio. Lencho called on Chucho to read from James 1:10-25. Chucho, his body wasted from a bout with tuberculosis, represented still another group of believers. His thin voice proclaimed these words:

> Do what God says, not just listening to him, not just deceiving yourselves. If a person hears God's Word and doesn't obey it, he is like a man looking into a mirror. He sees himself, then he goes away and right away forgets how he saw himself.

I hate deceit, Augustine thought. And self-deception is even worse. Why can't I use God's Word as a mirror to show up things in my life that don't please the Lord?

Finally, Lencho called on Tino to read from Romans chapter eight. Augustine watched his close friend as he took the large green Testament into his hands and spoke into the microphone. Certain words struck Augustine with renewed force:

> Those who have entered in with Christ Jesus are no longer condemned. They don't do the evil their livers beg for, but they do what the Holy Spirit wants. . . . He who keeps thinking about the evil his liver begs for will perish. But he who keeps thinking about doing

> what the Holy Spirit wants, that man will have life which doesn't end and he will have peace in his liver.

Augustine thanked God that Tino had sought him out long ago to walk with him in the Christian life. If only he could subdue the inner conflict that boiled within his own liver. He could be happy if he would obey the Holy Spirit.

He lowered his eyes uneasily and glanced at the throng of Popolucas who took in these words. He wondered how many would accept the new Bible and receive its message.

The ceremony drew to a close and the Bible Society director presented special copies of the New Testament to the town president, the judge, and to Lencho and his wife.

His name sounded over the loudspeaker. Augustine Roman, the brick and tile maker of long ago. Now the land commissioner. Between those years Christ remade him. He responded to his name. He rose to receive his copy and sat down.

At last he held the Book in his hands! He gazed at its luxurious green cover with his name engraved there in gold letters. The inscription on the inside front cover read:

> This book is presented to Augustine Roman in gratitude and in recognition for his valuable labor in the work of translation of the New Testament in the Popoluca language of Sayula.

The following day, Augustine leafed through the pages of the new Bible that spoke his language. He sat at a table in his home, the Testament open before him. "Lord," he prayed, "help me to balance the farm-union work with my spiritual life. I really want to devote myself to your words."

He stopped praying and listened. It seemed like every time he prayed the inevitable approach of steps came to interrupt. Next came the loud voice at the door and someone called his name.

Beto the merchant strode into the room, a triumphant smile on his face. He slapped a letter on the table. Not an ordinary letter. Government seals declared its importance.

"Auguch!" he cried. "Take a look at this. We've won. The governor is going to help us build the grain-storage bin."

Augustine snatched up the document, too amazed to believe what Beto had said. But it was true. The official letter bearing the governor's signature promised to help the Sayula people with their ambitious project.

During the following month Augustine's brain hummed like a nest of angry hornets—mornings at the town hall wrangling over legal problems, endless details to fill his mind as he directed construction. He found workers to clear the land, others to start the foundation work on the first building.

Evening hours found him slaving over bills, settling salaries for workmen, keeping accounts straight. And he worked alone. Farm officials patted him on the back and insisted he was the best man to direct the project.

Such overwhelming complexity threw Augustine into inner turmoil and he wondered when his brain would burst. But one month later the farm-union officials celebrated the first building erected at the edge of town.

"Good evening, Auguch." Lencho the Americano spoke to Augustine as he sprawled in a brightly colored hammock that stretched across the room. Augustine returned the greeting and pulled up a chair for his fellow translator. Gradually the conversation drifted to farm concerns.

"Ay, Lencho. I do have problems." His face tight with tension, Augustine rehearsed his troubles. "This farm project is the most important thing ever to happen for our people. I'm right in the middle of everything and everyone depends on me. But my term ends in three years and someone can take my place. Then I'll have more time to devote to the Lord."

Lencho started to speak, but steps sounded outside the door and another anxious rancher entered to ask Augustine for advice. As their conversation droned into the evening, Lencho finally stood up to leave. "I'm going now, Auguch. You know what you have to do. I'm leaving soon with my family, but we'll return in December. We'll pray that God will help you solve your problems."

The next two months sped by like gusts of wind while Augustine kept up his whirlwind schedule. As the grain-storage buildings rose, he made daily trips on his bicycle to inspect the work. One day in October he left the construction site early to get home to celebrate Tacho's birthday.

Climbing on his bicycle, he rode along a forest trail toward the asphalt highway that cut through his village. He looked back at the lot that held the grain-storage buildings. A dream was coming true and he felt good. The date was embedded in his mind: October 28, 1969—his son, Tacho, fifteen years old today. As he rode along, he felt assured that his boy would have a better life than he had had.

He crossed a ditch that ran alongside the highway. Tall weeds blocked his view, but the roar of oncoming trucks warned him to wait. Two trucks lumbered by, followed by some buses loaded with passengers. Several cars raced along and sharp blasts of wind forced Augustine to clutch his sombrero.

Silence settled over the highway and Augustine grew impatient. Pushing his bicycle up from the ditch, he mounted it and broke through the weeds onto the asphalt strip. He realized too late his mistake. A red pick-up bore down on him. Augustine dodged the vehicle but the violent rush of wind knocked him off balance and hurtled him into the ditch.

He lay stunned on the ground, his head throbbing violently. Gradually he staggered to his feet and surveyed the damage. One arm stung where deep scratches had been gouged into his skin above his shattered wristwatch. He looked in despair at his bicycle, now mangled beyond repair.

Augustine turned and forced himself along the rough path. He walked slowly, stopping often to still the trobbing in his head. The throbbing eased and he struck out on the closest trail for home. As he plodded along, thoughts of birthday parties disappeared from his mind and he wondered if he would have enough strength to get home. Finally he pushed open his door and dropped onto a cot.

He writhed in pain while his frightened wife and family clustered around him. Between the painful vibrations in his head he told in broken syllables of his accident. Gradually the pain subsided and some relief came.

The door flew open and his aunt, Ogo-Locha, burst into the room. She threw her arms around him. "Ay, Auguch," she said. "What happened, my son?"

Huge tears trickled down his cheeks. "Ay, Ogo-Locha, I nearly got killed."

As she consoled him, the pulsing in his head began to slow down. "God will take care of you," she said.

A flash of pain seared his mind and suddenly Augustine raised his right hand as though taking an oath. "I've had enough," he cried. He broke into convulsive sobs while his aunt embraced him. "I want God to take me. I'm ready to go anytime He says."

His father drew near the cot, his eyes worried, and he bowed his head in prayer. Augustine looked up at him. "Papa, why did it happen? Is God trying to show me something?"

Simon hesitated, then he spoke slowly. "Son, God *is* showing you something. You could have been killed, but your hour hasn't arrived yet. Instead He sent a sign. Who knows what it means?"

CHAPTER 19

The Rod that Stings

Augustine struggled out of the cot and pulled open the door. A new day in Sayula. He flipped the worn pages of a wall calendar until he found the date: Sunday, November 30, 1969. The year was nearly over.

The sky held a fringe of haze at the horizon. Another hot, humid day, Augustine thought. He tried to enjoy the morning but the dull ache in his brain returned to annoy him. The last thirty days since his accident pressed into his thoughts. They had dragged by slowly.

The pain had lingered and kept the memory of the accident throbbing in his mind. He remembered Beto, the worried storeowner, and his words: "We can't lose you, Auguch. You're right in the middle of our struggle. Someone else would ruin everything."

The doctors had found no brain damage. But why did he wake each morning with his mind scrambled, Augustine wondered, his thoughts muddled with pain.

A few callers came with difficult problems. They left and Augustine strode out of the yard. From the nearby church a cheerful hymn caught his attention. I should join them, he mused. But I've got to get relief from these callers. They don't even mind calling me out of church!

Land arguments churned in his mind, increasing the mental turmoil. The longing to escape urged him on his way.

He crossed the patio and found himself in his brother Anti's yard. Men clustered about the porch. He remembered why. St. Andrew's Day, Anti's birthday. Anti loved feasts, gave rum to his drinking buddies. I can't stay around these rumheads, Augustine thought. I've got to get away.

Sunday. A day of rest, Augustine thought ruefully. He walked the streets until the afternoon sun tore into his back like a branding iron. Celebrations haunted him. St. Andrew —a big saint. Everyone feasted to honor him. Popolucas born on this day bore Andrew's name and threw birthday parties.

Party crashers strolled into the yards like moths drawn to a lantern, preying on generous hosts. Custom dictated that everyone got something to eat—and drink.

Augustine moved on, his head throbbing, ready to burst. Men recognized him. "Hey, Auguch. Come here!" He was their friend—no blemish on their feast. Would the day ever drag to an end? No need to go home for lunch. Every birthday home dished up food. Augustine stopped to eat and drink with them. Custom hemmed him in.

His steps grew heavier. Forget about problems. Just enjoy the people—lie in the street when you get tired. The warm sun felt good on his neck. The street, yellow in the sunlight, looked longer and longer. Augustine quit the struggle, his legs buckled under him, and he fell beside the road.

Merrymakers ignored him as they rushed on to reach the next celebration. Let his family help him, they said.

At four that afternoon a woman's voice sounded in Augustine's head. He jolted awake and recognized Bella. She had come to help him find his way home. He walked the rough street with her, struggled down the path to his home, and sank onto a cot and fell asleep.

At six the wind caught the tune from a loudspeaker and funneled it into Augustine's ear. He jumped up and looked around him. A kerosene lamp threw orange rays into the room. Bella patted tortillas in the kitchen and his hungry children stuffed their mouths with beans and chunks of tortilla.

Reality flashed into his mind. He thought about the construction site. All that valuable equipment out there. It was his turn for guard duty!

He hurried around the room, washing his face, changing his shirt. The wooden trunk drew his attention and he threw it open. Bella came over to his side, her voice anxious.

"What are you looking for?"

Augustine rummaged in the trunk. "I need my revolver. Guard duty tonight."

"You're not well, Auguch. Come have supper." Bella pulled on his arm as though a warm meal would change his mind. "No one will bother that building."

"I'm responsible if anything is stolen." His voice bore the whetted edge of anger and Bella stepped back. He tossed out an old shirt and plunged his arms deeper into the trunk.

"Come have supper, please, Auguch. I'll find the gun. You're just making a mess."

Augustine turned toward the kitchen table but the thought of food repulsed him. Whirling around, he returned to the trunk. Bella, her fingers quicker than his, pulled out the holster with its revolver in place. He snatched it out of her hands and slung it around his waist.

"You don't need a gun," Bella said. "Everyone here is scared of the forest. No one will go near that building."

Augustine ignored her. He started toward the door but a glance into the kitchen arrested his attention and he stopped. He sized up the neighbor boy who sat in a dark corner. Joel, just eleven years old, wandered aimlessly around the village, dropped in on relatives, and idled away his time.

"Joel, you go with me," Augustine said. "Help me keep watch out there tonight."

A lopsided grin crossed the boy's face as though the idea sounded fun, something to ease the boredom of a dull Sunday evening. He jumped to his feet. "Sure, Auguch. Let's go."

"What good is that sour-brain kid?" Bella scolded. "His head is as hard as iron. Come have some supper."

Augustine shook his head. "We've got to go. It's dark already." He strode out into the night and Joel hurried after him.

A broad bar of light cut through the darkness from the open door of the church on the hill above him. Augustine looked at the church where believers had gathered for the evening service. The light triggered thoughts of God and he prayed, "Lord, I do trust in You and I want to follow You. Please bring this turmoil to an end."

His prayer ended, he headed on down the path. They trudged along a desolate road until they reached the crest of the hill overlooking the town. The way led through the forest and the shadows of giant trees plunged the trail into deeper darkness.

The boy released a gasp of fear. "I'm scared, Auguch."

Augustine felt the boy crowding close to him, his body trembling. "Don't worry, Joel. We'll be there soon. Let's hurry before robbers prey on the equipment."

Rounding a bend in the trail, the faint outline of the storage building came into view. Augustine drew near and flung open the door. Gradually his eyes adjusted to the dim interior. Everything looked fine. The worry that had kept him on edge vanished and drowsiness overcame him. He spread out a gunny sack and threw himself down.

"Joel, you wake me if you hear anyone coming."

The boy nodded in agreement. He kept up a stream of chatter until he realized no one was listening. Augustine was sound asleep.

An hour dragged by and Joel grew restless. This wasn't much fun, he thought, just sitting in a dark room with only a smoky kerosene lamp to exaggerate the darkness. His eyes played tricks on him. Sacks of cement and piles of grain looked like mute animals, their dark shapes grotesque in the night. Joel, bored with shapeless animals, began to watch Augustine as he lay on the ground.

Then he saw it. The holster that held Augustine's revolver stood out in sharp relief. Slowly Joel reached out his hand and touched the smooth leather. He expected Augustine to rise up and slap his hand. Augustine did not move. Joel unsnapped the holster and drew out the revolver.

A real gun! He had never held one before. The cold steel felt good and he rubbed the metal with his other hand.

Suddenly the revolver fired. A bang, a flash of light, a sharp cry of pain. The boy froze. Augustine raised up and then dropped heavily onto the dirt floor.

Terrified, the boy couldn't move, his senses numbed. Suddenly his legs urged him to run and he raced out the door. Shadows no longer frightened him as his feet tore along the grassy path. Jumbled ideas revolved in his mind—how to escape blame, who to tell. By the time he reached the edge of town an alibi formed in his mind.

He rushed up the street where the light still shone from the church. I don't dare tell them, he thought. They'll kill me. He dashed along the dark street until the light shining from Beto's general store came into view.

A surprised look spread over Beto's face as Joel lunged into the room—then a look of horror as the boy cried out the news.

"Beto! Come quickly! Auguch just shot himself!"

The alarm spread with lightning speed. A messenger broke up the church meeting with the startling news. Town loudspeakers shouted the message: "Augustine Roman in agony at the construction site."

Friends, relatives, the curious, all hurried along the forest trail. Beto arrived first at the building and looked in. Augustine lay stretched out on the floor. The storekeeper rushed in and threw his arms around him. "Auguch! What happened?"

The beat of rushing feet sounded in Beto's ears and he yelled at the first person who entered the building, "Get a taxi! And make sure that Joel kid goes along with us. We'll need his testimony."

The Roman family clustered around Augustine, their eyes straining in the dark to view the body, clutching for any signs of life. Bella, too frightened to enter, stood outside, trembling. Tacho drew near his father, his eyes filled with horror.

Augustine lay dying before them. He gave one final gasp of pain and whispered, "God, help me." His head flopped to the floor.

Outside, a man shouted, "We found a taxi. They'll take him to the hospital."

The cab raced along the asphalt strip and jerked to a halt in front of the hospital in Acayucan. Beto joined the paramedics as they rolled Augustine into the emergency ward. But the doctor looked at Augustine, shook his head and said, "You're too late. He's gone."

"He can't be dead." Beto stared at the doctor, refusing to believe him. A few hours before, Augustine had been at home. Earlier Beto had seen him strolling around the village. Slowly the truth dawned on the storekeeper. It was true. Augustine was gone. The Roman family was waiting in the hospital corridor. How could he tell them? Finally he steeled himself and walked out of the emergency room.

The steel turned to clay as Beto approached the family. He remembered Bella's timidity in the face of death but he knew Tacho and Simon stood nearby to console her. He broke the news. Stunned by the sudden loss, the trio nodded, and tears rolled down their cheeks.

Simon spoke first. "Well, his hour arrived. We'll take him back to Sayula and bury him."

"Not yet," Beto said. "A shooting death demands an autopsy. They have to investigate."

The evening wore on. When Beto emerged from the operating room, he shook his head. "It wasn't suicide. The bullet entered from the left side. Augustine was right-handed. He couldn't have shot himself. We told the Joel kid what we found out and he broke down and told the truth."

CHAPTER 20

The Word Still Speaks

Chompa stared at the people as they crowded into the streets. His eyes misted with tears and he brushed them away with a sweep of the hand.

You're a man, he told himself firmly. Only women weep.

One exception, he reminded himself. Men cry when drunk, let their emotions rage, let the tears flow. But the "cooked water" belonged to his past life. A new life embraced him and made him resist the urge to turn to liquor to dull the terrible loss he felt.

Augustine gone! Chompa braced himself against the door of his hut and this time he let the tears flow. Mexican law demanded burial within twenty-four hours after a death. It was Monday afternoon. Chompa broke away from his hut and began to plod along behind the procession that bore Augustine's casket.

As the pallbearers marched on, Popoluca men and women left their houses and joined the procession. Stores and saloons lost customers and the owners closed their doors and went along. By the time they reached the graveyard at the edge of town, the procession had swollen to a throng.

Chompa stopped at the gate to the graveyard. The former alcoholic wore wrinkled jeans with a denim shirt that hung in tatters around his shoulders. Most of the mourners had donned their best clothes. A sense of unworthiness overwhelmed him and he was turning to leave when suddenly a friendly hand touched his shoulder and he whirled around.

"Simon!" Chompa felt a wave of gratitude wash over him as Augustine's father came along beside him. "Look at this crowd."

Simon whispered in amazement. "I've never seen so many people at a funeral. The whole town is here."

"Sure they're here," Chompa said. He nodded toward a group of farmers who clustered around a freshly dug grave. "Those men won't forget Augustine."

"Let's go over there," Simon urged, and he pulled on Chompa's arm.

More than fifty farmers mingled with Augustine's family at the grave site. His older brother Lino stood in front of the crowd. With vocal cords loosened by rum he pronounced a fiery discourse in praise of his brother. Words caught in his throat and he sobbed, crying out, "Augustine! Augustine!" as though he would call him back from the dead. Finally he convulsed in tears.

The crowd at the grave shifted their feet impatiently as if they were merely enduring Lino's outburst and they looked relieved when Beto stepped forward. The town merchant owned a loudspeaker and his voice was familiar to the people. Gifted in eloquent speech from years of announcing celebrations, he started to proclaim what Augustine had meant to the farm program in Sayula.

"Friends," Beto said, "let us never forget that Augustine struggled and died for us."

Suddenly he choked up and his words came to a halt. Tears welled in his eyes and he looked around for someone else to speak. He lit a cigarette and puffed in silence while Balbino, the town butcher, spoke.

Only five feet tall, stocky, with thick graying hair, Balbino had the authoritative look of someone more imposing than the local meat man. He took his turn to speak more words of praise in memory of Augustine.

Chu-Odi stepped forward to add his remarks. Tall, thin as a string, he seemed to sway in the wind as he spoke. "Farm leaders die violent deaths," he observed, and he recited an impressive list of local heroes who had died for their convictions. "Let's keep on striving for our land rights," he said, his voice cracking with emotion.

Chompa listened and gradually the fire returned to his eyes. What about the Lord? he wondered. Don't these farmers realize that Christ made Augustine what he was? He hesitated. They wouldn't listen to a former drunk—the man who once urged Augustine to drink with him, who had teased him and mocked him. Would these people believe old Chompa had really changed?

The speeches ended and the band of farm laborers stared at the grave which held their leader. Chompa drew alongside Balbino. His steps faltered. As a drunk he had been brash. He had felt no shame barging into a room full of people and disturbing everyone. Rum had been the magic genie that helped him blunder through life. Now he was stone sober—and helpless. Unless God helped him.

"Listen, Balbino," he said. As he spoke the eyes of the farm workers turned toward him and he sensed how they disdained him. "I've got something to say about Augustine."

Balbino turned his gaze on Beto, the one most likely to lead them now that Augustine was gone. Chompa stared at the ground, praying, hoping they would let him talk.

Beto looked at Chompa. Then he eyed Augustine's family—Tacho, the wife Bella, and especially the staunch father Simon, who bore the loss of his son like a stoic. Simon returned Beto's gaze and nodded his head as if to say, It's all right. Let him talk.

"Very well," Beto said with a shrug as he looked again at Chompa. "Augustine meant a lot to you, didn't he?"

Chompa sensed the Holy Spirit encouraging him to speak, to take what could be his last chance to address an audience like Beto and his men, who had come to the graveyard out of respect for Augustine.

"Augustine was my cousin," Chompa replied. "Ten years younger than me. But he was older than me in many ways. I was like a nursing child. I nursed on booze!"

The remark drew guffaws from the crowd but only a thin smile played on Beto's lips. The smile failed to disguise the annoyed look in his eyes. Lino's speech had rambled too long. Why let alcoholics prolong the day with incoherent speeches? He looked helplessly at Simon but the old man nodded his head again and smiled. Beto folded his arms and waited for Chompa to finish.

"Augustine was beyond many of us," Chompa continued. "I once taught him to drink. Now I'm ashamed of myself. Christ took hold of him and then He grabbed me too." Chompa clenched his fist and held it out. "He holds me tight. Now I'm growing up, learning to walk like a child. Many of us in Augustine's family now trust this marvelous Christ. We invite you to hear the Word of God and trust Him too."

Chompa stepped back into the crowd. Every eye was trained on the town merchant.

Beto cleared his throat. "Friends, we should hear what Augustine believed. God's message was important to him and that makes it important to us. We've heard this short word from someone whom Augustine has helped. He helped us, too. Let's visit Augustine's family and comfort them in their grief. And, yes, let's respect the Word of God, just as our leader, Augustine, did."

The farmers nodded in approval and Balbino slapped Chompa on the back. "Nice going!" he said. "Let us know when you have meetings. We want to come."

Would they? Chompa didn't know if they would come. But the morning hours which had dragged began to pick up momentum as hope surged. He looked out over the people. Believers mingled with the crowd, almost lost among the farmers. His son, Lash, stood with them, his face shining with hope. He had wanted a Popoluca New Testament more than any of the others and he paid for his copy two weeks in advance.

Chompa remembered with gratitude how Lash had read the Scriptures to him many years ago. Gradually the seed had sprung up in Lash's life until days of bitterness arrested his spiritual growth. But Lash had recovered, remarried and was seeking the Lord again. All he wanted now was more of God's Word.

As the morning turned into afternoon, the people began their trek back to their homes. Chompa strode toward Augustine's home, rejoicing. The people had wanted a strong leader to help them with their problems. Augustine was their man, but Christ had made him strong, made him capable to lead. Now Augustine was gone, taken in the prime of life. But, Chompa thought, only Christ can free us from the clutches of Satan and put us into God's hand. Then we are truly free.

Chompa drew near to Augustine's home just as the last light of the day was vanishing. The words that had sounded in his mind that morning came rushing back: Augustine was gone. Now he corrected himself. Augustine is not gone, he said to himself. What he did for me and for the rest of his people can't die that easily. And now he is with the Lord.

Simon's quiet voice broke into Chompa's reverie. He was standing by the trail where he often stood to watch the sun set. "Hey, Chompa. Get down to Bella's house. The tamales are hot. And Lencho the Americano just arrived from Mexico City. He's down there and wants to chat with us."

"Lencho? I wondered if he was coming back. He missed the whole funeral—burial and all."

"We shocked him with the news about Augustine. He wants to read some Scripture with us."

Chompa and Simon worked their way down the steps carved in the limestone and entered the house where Augustine had lived with his family. Lencho rose from his stool and gave them a warm handshake. Bella unwrapped tamales and placed them on the table in front of the men. They ate slowly, as if they couldn't taste what they were eating. Tacho, his eyes still swollen from grief, sat with them. They wanted to talk about the death of his father.

"Only God knows why it happened," Simon said. "His hour had arrived."

"It wasn't just his hour," Tacho said. "God had a purpose in it. My father was busy in the farm work, busy helping people. The whole job was too big for him but he wanted to do it—even if he worked day and night."

Lencho nodded in agreement. "I think of that verse in Romans 8:28, the way we translated it into Popoluca. Do you have the New Testament here, Tacho?"

Tacho threw open the trunk and pulled out the green book—Augustine's special copy—and handed it to Lencho.

"I see you have your father's Bible," Lencho said.

"Yes," Tacho replied, his voice strong with determination.

"I plan to use it all the time. I promised God I'd never go back on Him."

Simon's voice held a hint of regret. "Augustine lived only a few months after you gave him that book. And too busy to read it much. I wonder how much good it did him."

Lencho smiled. "It did him plenty of good. For ten years we worked on that New Testament and its message gave Augustine the courage to serve his people." He leafed through the pages of the green book until Romans 8:28 fell open before him. He read aloud the words:

> We know that in everything that happens to us, God is causing us to turn out well because we love Him, because God called us to do his will.

"Nothing happens by chance," Lencho said. "God works in every situation. Tacho, everyone I meet wants to talk about your father. They all speak well of him."

Simon broke in. "He fought for his people because he wanted them to live better. They won't say anything bad about him."

"That's right," Lencho said. "And each time we go from house to house with this New Testament, we'll remind the Sayula people that Augustine had a tremendous part in the translation. God won't forget the work we do out of love for Him. Augustine's deepest desire was that his people would come to know his Lord. He knew that only God's Word in their language would help them."

While the men talked, Chompa remained silent. Sayula people had nicknamed him Old Dirty Mouth because foul and obscene talk once poured from his mouth like a broken sewer line. He was learning to keep his mouth shut and to listen to God's Word. But as Tacho and Lencho spoke, words began to burn.

"Ay, Lencho," Chompa said, "I'm going to talk now. Do you realize two blind men are in this room?"

Chompa's voice erupted into a sharp laugh as Lencho's face drew a blank. He loved to tease and he hoped some merriment would begin to erase the sorrow of the day that had gone by. "Two blind men are here, Lencho," he explained. "Simon and I are blind."

"Your eyes look fine to me. But remember, Chompa, I'm

an outsider. Tell me what you mean."

"I mean we can't read. Simon and I never learned. We had to work in the fields when we were young. There were no schools. That's why we listen. We learn by hearing God's Word."

He turned to Tacho. "You're still young and you've learned to read. You can make the paper speak. Read clearly so blind men can listen to God's Word."

"That's right," Lencho said. "Some of the older people may never learn to read. But they can keep their ears open to God's message." Lencho looked at his watch. "It's getting late and I've got to get home to my family."

"Well," Chompa said, "if you're going, then go. I've got my family here—right over there in the corner." He pointed to a stack of corn piled high against the wall. "That's my family," he said with a chuckle. "We two blind men will shell corn while Tacho reads to us. OK, Tacho?"

When Lencho left, the family sat in silence, still numb from sorrow. Then Bella went back to patting out tortillas. Simon and Chompa pulled over a basket and began shelling corn. And Tacho stretched out in the hammock and opened the pages of the green book that spoke his language. He began to read.

Afterword

The farmers did come to the chapel. But two years later.

On November 30, 1971, the farm workers met at Augustine's grave. The passage of time had not erased the memory of their leader. They came to honor Augustine for all he had done in fighting for their rights.

After the speeches were made, as the Americano who worked with Augustine on the Popoluca Scriptures, I invited them to a memorial service that evening to hear Augustine's testimony. We had a cassette tape that he had recorded during the final check on the New Testament.

That evening the same farmers who had stood at Augustine's graveside filled the seats of the chapel. They had told others. A hundred men packed to overflowing the rustic meeting hall which was built to accommodate thirty people.

Their faces grew alert when the voice of their leader echoed through the chapel and via loudspeaker out over the village. They heard Augustine's testimony, how God had delivered him and many of his family from darkness. I trusted that those who listened would discover God's salvation for themselves.

Beto the merchant came that night—for the first time. He had said to the farmers, "God's message was important to Augustine and that makes it important to us." He listened to Augustine's testimony and only God knows how the seed of the Word will grow in Beto's life.

The growth of the Word in the lives of the Poplucas has been gradual. But over the past fifteen years, since 1972, many people have been touched and changed through the translated message from God.

Felix had no interest in the Gospel when we lived in his village. When I visited the region in 1980, Felix came up and said, "I want you to know I'm a believer now. I put my trust in Christ and now I'm baptized. The way of the Lord is the only way to go."

I once despaired for Panuncio, my first language helper in 1954. He became a schoolteacher and lost interest in the Gospel. Later, his mind confused by materialistic educators, he nearly ruined his life with a drinking problem. Now Panuncio has come back to the Lord and talks about God's greatness.

One Popoluca family seemed hopeless. Chala lived in a ramshackle hut with her family. Her husband died an alcoholic and the children accepted a careless life-style. One son, Pedro, lay around in his hammock, his life without meaning. What a joy, therefore, to have him stroll into our home one afternoon. He was dressed in new clothes and a straw hat topped an alert face now gleaming with hope.

Pedro asked me for a Popoluca New Testament and told of his plans to get baptized as a new believer in Christ. "I want to wash away my old sins," he said. God had worked in a sovereign way in Pedro's life and now he rejoices in the Lord.

The Gospel in Popoluca has also spread through the family unit. Chompa had many sons and space permitted mention only of Lash. But another son was growing up who has astounded us with his growth in the Lord.

Moises Roman was only thirteen when the Popoluca New Testament was presented to his people. But three years later he was eager to help record the entire New Testament onto cassette tapes.

One February day in 1972 a relentless noonday sun blazed down on the tropical Indian village of Sayula. Moises and I trudged along the highway until we swung off into a cool path that led between shade trees and hiked to a ranch where a Christian couple lives. There we recorded the book of Jude and the first three chapters of Mark's Gospel.

At four in the afternoon we pounded the trail back to Sayula. The highway seemed like a huge griddle that was getting hotter and hotter as we walked along it. But Moises, just sixteen years old and used to the heat, chatted about the cassettes. He wanted his people to hear the Word of God.

His parents, Chompa and Macha, were eager to hear what we had recorded. We started the cassette player and they listened intently. Neighbors heard their own language on the machine and also stopped and listened. By the time four chapters of the Scriptures had been played, a spontaneous congregation stood in the yard, listening. Now we have the New Testament on tape and cassette players in Christian homes. Popolucas who can't or won't read the New Testament can at least hear it. Many who won't go to church will listen to four or five chapters of the Bible.

We left the land of the Popolucas in 1980 and have not returned. What is happening now?

Recently, a man rang the bell to the group house in Mexico City where the Bible translators live. He looked like a Mexican with his dark hair and olive complexion but his clothes were rumpled from an all-night bus ride. He had traveled four hundred miles out of the steamy lowlands of Veracruz to come to the city.

It was Tino. He asked if someone could supply him with copies of the Popoluca New Testament. "We are still meeting around the Word of God," Tino reported. "We gather together to study the Scriptures and we sill use the Popoluca New Testament in the services."

Tino, one of the first to trust in the Lord when I arrived in Sayula in 1954, took three years to win Augustine to the Lord. But he never gave up on his boyhood friend. When Augustine trusted in Christ, the seed of the Word sprouted in his family and one by one they came to know the Lord. That work of God continues to this day as one by one the Popolucas are hearing the Scriptures and trusting in Christ.

Letters still reach me from Sayula village. A young school teacher wrote and asked me for copies of the New Testament. He has trusted in the Lord and longs to learn more about Christ.

"God is winning more souls in our family," he wrote. "Now

in addition to my parents, two of my sisters and a brother go with me to church. I'm learning much of the Bible and gradually I am understanding the reason for our existence here on earth. Every night before going to sleep, I pray and give thanks to our Creator for giving to me another day of life. Also I ask God to help me day by day in my work."

I never met this fellow when I lived in Sayula. He is the result of the seed of the Word. It has been planted and now it springs up and God is harvesting his people from among the Popolucas.

One wayward youth brought Augustine's life to an end. Joel, because he was a minor, was never tried for the shooting. He was a distant relative of Augustine, and the Roman clan out of family loyalty never pressed charges. But Chompa and other Christians see beyond Augustine's death and realize he is not really gone. He still serves his people through the New Testament in their language. The translated message from God stands as a triumphant witness to the faith of this one Popoluca man.

Fear. Custom. Noise. Each challenged God's revelation of Himself in Christ to the Popolucas. But light has broken through the darkness for Popoluca men and women. And it has not been silent.

Simon Roman (r.) stands proudly with his children (r. to l. in order of birth), Lino (eldest), Andres, Faustina, Ruperto, Augustine, Filemon and Anastacio.

Bella and Augustine with their children (l. to r.), Tacho, Marta, Samuel and Claudio.

A big smile graces Augustine's face as Lash (second from left) and other family and friends gather for Easter Sunrise service at Tino's ranch.

Augustine (l.), his home now big enough, enjoys a gospel meeting along with family members like (r. to l.) Lash, Chompa and Simon.

Augustine takes translation work seriously in Mexico City.

Tile-roofed houses are popular in modern Sayula.

Tino (l.) and Augustine pitch in to repair a mud wall.

Many hands made a mud and bamboo wall rise quickly.

The machete is a handy tool to scrape broom corn before making new brooms.

The old versus the new. Ogo-Locha learns to live around modern Volkswagen beetles.

Augustine scrutinizes the Popoluca book of Acts, while cousin Tomasa looks at her own copy.

Back in 1954, two Americanos, Morgan Whittaker (l.) and Larry Clark found the new highway through Veracruz an exciting adventure.

In 1954 the bells tolled the hour from an ancient church that graced the village square in Sayula.

A sea of old houses and tropical green greeted the eye in 1954.

Augustine (r.) finds the Americano's house rather quaint as he works with Lencho on translation.

The old way is better. Simon gets right into the mud as he mixes grass for plastering the bamboo walls.